GLOBAL ORGANIZATIONS

The Arab League

D0465262

GLOBAL ORGANIZATIONS

The African Union

The Arab League

The Association of Southeast Asian Nations

The Caribbean Community and Common Market

The European Union

The International Atomic Energy Agency

The Organization of American States

The Organization of Petroleum
Exporting Countries

The United Nations

The United Nations Children's Fund

The World Bank and
the International Monetary Fund

The World Health Organization

The World Trade Organization

GLOBAL ORGANIZATIONS

The Arab League

Cris E. Toffolo

Series Editor
Peggy Kahn
University of Michigan–Flint

Clifton Park - Halfmoon Public Library
475 Moe Road
Clifton Park, New York 12065

CHELSEA HOUSE
PUBLISHERS
An imprint of Infobase Publishing

Chelsea House
An imprint of Infobase Publishing
132 West 31st Street
New York NY 10001

1354

Library of Congress Cataloging-in-Publication Data

Toffolo, Cris E.
Global organizations: The Arab League / Cris E. Toffolo.
   p. cm.
Includes bibliographical references and index.
ISBN: 978-0-7910-9565-2 (hardcover)
 1. League of Arab States—Juvenile literature. 2. Arab countries—Juvenile literature.
I. Title.

DS36.2.T64 2008
341.24'77—dc22   2007042706

Chelsea House books are available at special discounts when purchased in bulk quantities for businesses, associations, institutions, or sales promotions. Please call our Special Sales Department in New York at (212) 967-8800 or (800) 322-8755.

You can find Chelsea House on the World Wide Web at http://www.chelseahouse.com

Series design by Erik Lindstrom
Cover design by Ben Peterson

Printed in the United States of America

Bang KT 10 9 8 7 6 5 4 3 2 1

This book is printed on acid-free paper.

All links and Web addresses were checked and verified to be correct at the time of publication. Because of the dynamic nature of the Web, some addresses and links may have changed since publication and may no longer be valid.

CONTENTS

1

Introduction to the League of Arab States

THE LEAGUE OF ARAB STATES (ARABIC: *AL-JAMI'A AD-DUWAL al-Arabiyah*), or Arab League (*Al-Jamai'a al-Arabiyah*)—the league or AL for short—is a regional organization established in 1945. Unlike other regional organizations founded on geography, such as the European Union (EU), the league is based on a shared culture, rooted in a common language (Arabic). It was set up to help Arab countries coordinate their policies, gain a united political voice in the world, and develop a better common future together. Its charter provides for the coordination of political, educational, financial, legal, security, cultural, social, and communications affairs. It is also charged with co-coordinating business relationships, passports, and health issues.

The organization provides a place in which decisions can be made at a level above the individual states that are its members. It tries to prevent the domination of Arab countries from the outside. It also seeks to replace rivalries between member countries with cooperative relationships, so that members can all develop more quickly and in a way that helps the whole group. The league's secretary-general since 2001 is Amr Moussa, and he has been popular in the region. He is committed to using the institutions that the league has developed over the past 60 years, and maybe some new ones, to help ordinary people in their everyday lives.

WHO ARE ARABS?

Arabs are people whose language is Arabic, who live in Arabic-speaking countries and are sympathetic to the aspirations of Arabic-speaking peoples. The Arab world (*al-'alam al-'arabi*) is defined by this shared language, shared historical experience, and common way of life.

The 22 countries in the Arab League have a population of about 317 million, which is slightly larger than the population of the United States (about 300 million). The region's average gross domestic product per person (GDP per capita), which is a measure of an economy's ability to produce goods and services, is $7,890 per person, though it varies a lot within states and between states. The GDP has been growing at an average of 5.6 percent a year for the past five years, and in 2006 it is estimated that together the Arab countries' economy is worth about $1 trillion (the United States' is $13.2 trillion), putting them 10th in the world in terms of combined GDP. The league, therefore, represents an economically powerful segment of the world.

Since the late nineteenth century, the term *Arab* has also been an important way for people to identify themselves politically. People in this region started to see themselves as sharing many common traits as well as many common problems. They believed that Arabs should have their own independent nation-state in the territory of what was then officially part of the Ottoman Empire (even though real control of the area was in the hands of Great Britain and France). This powerful idea about having an Arab state is called Arab nationalism. This idea is behind the formation of the league.

WHICH COUNTRIES ARE IN THE ARAB LEAGUE?

All Arab countries are members of the league, even those which lie outside of the Middle East and North Africa (MENA). When it was founded on March 22, 1945, the league had seven members: Egypt, Syria, Lebanon, Iraq, Trans-Jordan (now called Jordan), Saudi Arabia, and Yemen. At that time, the Palestinians (Arabs from Palestine) were given founding status, with full voting rights, even though they lacked any independent state of their own. In the 1970s, the Palestine Liberation Organization (PLO) became the Palestinians' voting representative in the league.

Other states joined the league as they gained political independence or began to see advantages to membership. As of early 2008, there are 22 voting members. In 2003, Eritrea, which is an Arab country, joined as an observer, which means it can attend league meetings but cannot vote. Since then the league has opened up observer status to non-Arab states as well. This has led to the following countries joining as observers: Armenia (2004); Chad (2005); Turkey (2005); Venezuela (2006); and India (2007). It is likely that Russia and perhaps Iran will also soon join as observers.

PHYSICAL GEOGRAPHY

League member countries cover about 8.38 million square miles (13.5 million square kilometers), an area that is about one and a third times the size of the United States' 6.08 million

(continues on page 12)

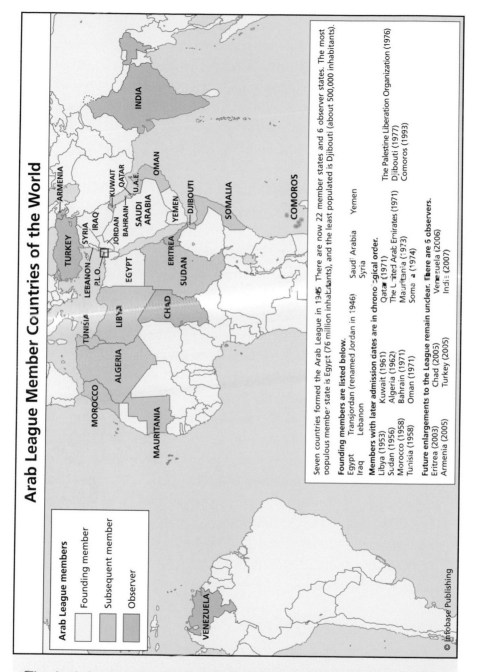

Arab League Member Countries of the World

Arab League members

☐ Founding member
▨ Subsequent member
▨ Observer

Seven countries formed the Arab League in 1945. There are now 22 member states and 6 observer states. The most populous member state is Egypt (76 million inhabitants), and the least populated is Djibouti (about 500,000 inhabitants).

Founding members are listed below.

| Egypt | Transjordan (renamed Jordan in 1946) | Saudi Arabia | Yemen |
| Iraq | Lebanon | Syria | |

Members with later admission dates are in chronological order.

Libya (1953)	Kuwait (1961)	Qatar (1971)	The United Arab Emirates (1971)	The Palestine Liberation Organization (1976)
Sudan (1956)	Algeria (1962)	The United Arab Emirates (1971)	Mauritania (1973)	Djibouti (1977)
Morocco (1958)	Bahrain (1971)	Mauritania (1973)		Comoros (1993)
Tunisia (1958)	Oman (1971)	Somalia (1974)		

Future enlargements to the League remain unclear. There are 5 observers.

| Eritrea (2003) | Chad (2005) | Venezuela (2006) |
| Armenia (2005) | Turkey (2005) | India (2007) |

© Infobase Publishing

The Arab League was created with seven members with the goal of promoting both Arab unity and the interests of member states. Today there are 22 members and 6 observers.

MEMBERS OF THE ARAB LEAGUE

COUNTRY NAME	JOINING DATE	DATE OF INDEPENDENCE	POPULATION (THOUSANDS)
Algeria	1962	1962	32,930
Bahrain	1971	1971	699
Comoros	1993	1975	691
Djibouti	1977	1977	487
Egypt	1945	1922	78,887
Iraq	1945	1932	26,783
Jordan	1945	1946	5,907
Kuwait	1961	1961	2,418
Lebanon	1945	1943	3,874
Libya	1953	1960	5,901
Mauritania	1973	1960	3,177
Morocco	1958	1956	33,241
Oman	1971	1650	3,102
Palestine	1945	N/A	N/A
Qatar	1971	1971	885
Saudi Arabia	1945	1932	27,020
Somalia	1974	1960	8,863
Sudan	1956	1956	41,236
Syria	1945	1946	1,888
Tunisia	1958	1956	10,175
UAE*	1971	1971	2,603
Yemen	1945	1990**	21,456
TOTAL	317,009		

* United Arab Emirates

** Date the country reunited

Source: *The World Fact Book Database*, Central Intelligence Agency of the United States, July 2007.

(continued from page 9)

square miles (9.8 million square kilometers.). Its western edge extends to the Atlantic Ocean; to the north it reaches the Mediterranean Sea; and to the east, it abuts the Persian Gulf, the Gulf of Oman, the Arabian Sea, and the Indian Ocean.

Many League countries are in an area commonly referred to as the Middle East. This term was first used by Europeans

ARABS & MUSLIMS— WHAT'S THE DIFFERENCE?

The term *Arab* refers to people who speak Arabic and come from the Middle East and North Africa. Most Arabs share common cultural values such as respect for family, honor, and hospitality. They also share many historical experiences and common interests.

Muslims are followers of Islam, the world's fastest-growing religion. In 2007 the number of Muslims in the world was estimated to be 1.39 billion, about 21 percent of the world's population of 6.6 billion people.* The word *Islam* in Arabic means "submission" and refers to obedience to God (Arabic: *Allah*). Islam's holy book is the Qur'an. Muslims date the founding of Islam to A.D. 622, which is Year One of the Islamic calendar. This is the date of the *Hijra* (migration), when Islam's founder, the Prophet Muhammad, left Mecca for Medina.

The two dominant strains of Islam are Sunnism and Shi'ism (roughly 85 percent and 15 percent of all Muslims, respectively). The division between these groups dates to the earliest days of Islam and developed from a conflict over who should lead the community. Over time, other differences—such as legal traditions and holidays—have also developed. Shi'as are a majority of the population in only four Muslim countries: Iran (89 percent of all Muslims), Bahrain (70 percent), Iraq (65 percent), and Azerbaijan (80 percent). They constitute 60 percent of Lebanon's Muslims, but Muslims compose only 60 percent of that country's population.

to describe the region that lay to the east of Europe. Today, people in the region debate the name of the area in which they live. Some refer to it as the "Arab world," while others think this term refers only to the Arabian Peninsula. People in the Maghreb (northwestern Africa) don't really feel that the term refers to them. Some prefer the term "Islamic world," but others

Most Arabs are Muslims. In fact, 90 percent of all Arabs are Muslim, and most of these are Sunni Muslims. The remaining 10 percent of the Arab population is largely Christian. For instance, 10 percent of the populations of Egypt and Syria is Christian.

Until the creation of the Jewish state of Israel, it was not uncommon to talk about "Jewish Arabs," who either had been in the region since the origin of Judaism or had returned after being expelled from Spain in 1492 and then were given refuge by the Ottoman Empire. Today, almost all Jewish Arabs have moved to Israel—and given the bitter conflicts between Arab states and Israel, Jewish Arab identity is no longer accepted by either Arabs or Jews.

Most Muslims are *not* Arabs: Arabs make up only about 20 percent of all Muslims. This means that out of the world's 1.32 billion Muslims, only about 264 million are Arabs. None of the world's four largest Muslim countries are ethnically Arab: Indonesia (213 million); Pakistan (157 million); India (144 million); and Bangladesh (122 million). Egypt, which has 71 million Muslims, is the only Arab country with a large total population.

* Central Intelligence Agency of the United States, *The World Fact Book*. Available online at *https://www.cia.gov/library/publications/the-world-factbook/geos/xx.html#People*.

are cautious about using this term since today most Muslims live in other regions of the world. Thus by default, many people refer to their area as the Middle East or as the Middle East and North Africa (MENA), which is how the area is referred to by the United Nations.

Morocco, Algeria, Tunisia, and Libya are the member states in the Maghreb (Arabic for "the land where the sun sets"). Several other members are located in northeastern Africa, also known as the Horn of Africa. They are Eritrea (observer), Sudan, and Somalia. Two other members are archipelagos (groups of islands). These are Bahrain, located in the Gulf of Bahrain, which is part of the Persian Gulf, and the Comoros, located in the Indian Ocean, just off of the east coast of Africa, north of the island of Madagascar.

THE ISLAMIC RENAISSANCE

The most glorious periods in Arab history occurred during some of Islam's greatest eras. These eras spanned the period of time from the seventh to the thirteenth centuries. The first of these, called the Golden Age of Islam, covers the lifetime of the Prophet Muhammad plus the next 40 years when the Muslim community was led by the "first four rightly guided caliphs," who were all companions of the Prophet. Muslims believe that during this period, the community had missionary zeal and a clear sense of humanity and justice.

The second great Islamic period (A.D. 656–750), which directly follows the first, is that of the Umayyad Empire. This Sunni Arab empire was the largest political entity in the world at the time. Islamic rule extended far beyond the Arabian Peninsula, across North Africa into Spain in the west, and to Afghanistan and parts of India in the east. The Umayyads moved their capital to Damascus, which today is the capital of Syria.

The downfall of the Umayyads came when non-Arab Shi'a groups became unhappy with Arab control of the empire. These

Shi'a groups rallied around Abbas, a descendant of the Prophet's uncle, and overthrew the Umayyads. The Shi'a Abbasids ushered in a third Islamic golden age, which coincided with the European Dark Ages. The Abbasids established their capital in Baghdad and turned this city into the most important center of learning outside of China. They preserved Greek and Roman philosophy and science and made advances in these fields, as well as in many others. The Abbasid Empire ended when it was overrun by the Mongols in A.D. 1250.

The last great Islamic empire in this region was the Ottoman, known for its innovative military and bureaucratic systems and for great works of art. It reached its zenith in the middle of the sixteenth century under Suleyman the Magnificent. During the eighteenth and nineteenth centuries, however, at a time when European weapons and travel technologies were advancing, the Ottoman governing structures were no longer dynamic and lost the ability to effectively control the empire's vast territory. As a result of these developments, newer European imperial powers—particularly the British and the French—pushed their way into the region and developed governing relationships that subordinated local Arab people.

As in North America, sometimes this entailed direct colonial rule that included European peoples moving into the territory (e.g., the French in Algeria allowed poor French farmers to establish farms on land taken from the local people). In other places, Europeans directly colonized an area simply to use and/or extract its resources (e.g., the French in Lebanon). Still another method of control was used in Egypt, where the French under Napoleon, and then the British, determined events but pretended the Ottoman Empire was still in control. (This is sometimes referred to as "double-decker" colonialism, a reference to the red double-decker buses that are a hallmark of London, the center of the British Empire.)

Suleyman I the Magnificent (1494–1566) is considered the greatest of the Ottoman sultans. During his reign, the Ottoman Empire reached its peak in power and prosperity. He is known for renovating the empire's legal and economic system, sponsoring the arts and architecture, and supporting educational reform. At the time of his death, the Ottoman Empire's territories included most of the Balkans, northern Africa, and the Middle East, and it controlled the trade routes on the Mediterranean Sea.

The British used a similar form of indirect rule in the "Trucial States" of the southwestern Persian Gulf, many of which are now united into the United Arab Emirates (UAE). There the British signed truces with local leaders in 1820. Under these agreements, local rulers ran daily affairs but all foreign relationships were controlled by Great Britain so that it could maintain control of its empire in India by controlling the trade routes to it.

The major wars of the twentieth century all greatly impacted this region. After World War I, which ended the Ottoman Empire, the region's political map was redrawn, and in the process the seeds of future conflicts were sown. During World War I, the British made conflicting promises to the Arabs, French, and Jews. Although political independence was promised to Arabs in exchange for their cooperation with the Entente powers (including Great Britain, France, and the United States) against the Central powers (including Germany, Austria, and the Ottoman Empire), in most cases these promises were not kept until after World War II.

Following World War II, the world was dominated by the Cold War—a conflict between the United States and the Soviet Union (USSR) that lasted from the mid-1940s until 1991. While it never resulted in direct combat between these two superpowers, their deeply hostile relationship produced a nuclear arms race and many "hot wars" between their smaller dependent allies (client states). Arab states were pressured by both superpowers to become loyal clients, and this contributed to the difficulties that the league had in coming to agreement on key issues.

New divisions developed within the league in 1990 when Iraq invaded Kuwait, which are both league members. Other members disagreed about how to respond to Iraq's aggression, especially about whether to support involvement by the

United States and other non-Arab states. The 2003 U.S. invasion of Iraq has led to further problems, in part because it has brought out the region's Sunni-Shi'a division. In addition, one of President George W. Bush's stated reasons for going to war is to spread democracy and to have Arab countries support democratic rulers. This is a controversial proposition because some Arab governments are monarchies (where a king rules) or authoritarian regimes (where a dictator rules) and many others, though officially democratic regimes, are governed by autocratic leaders who don't always play by democratic rules. The existence of these different types of regimes complicates the politics of the league because they are based on different principles and pursue different goals. These, in turn, result in clashes within the league.

THE ARAB LEAGUE'S OBJECTIVES

The league was one of the first regional organizations, established in March 22, 1945, before World War II ended and even before the official founding of the United Nations on October 24, 1945. It grew out of the idea of Arab nationalism (also called Pan-Arabism) which holds that Arabs must stand together in order to stop continued European domination. From this perspective, it is not surprising that within five years of its founding, the league's members wrote the Joint Defense and Economic Cooperation Treaty (JDEC), which committed them to come to one another's aid when attacked from outside, and to refrain from using arms against one another.

From this angle it is also possible to see why the establishment of Israel in 1948—only three years after the founding of the league and years before many parts of the Arab world gained independence from European colonial rule—is such a major issue on which the league regularly takes action. Whereas many Jews saw Israel as their rightful homeland, and many in the West, including Jews, saw the formation of Israel as a necessary response to the Holocaust, Arabs' historical experience told them that the creation of Israel, after decades of their objections, was just another extension of Western colonial domination. They saw it as another example of the West's long practice of using Arab resources (in this case, land) to solve one of its own problems (the need to atone for Germany's murder of 6 million Jews). Once again the Arabs believed they would suffer.

While Western news media still usually speak about the Arab-Israel conflict as one big problem, today the reality is much more complex. It includes the issue of whether the Palestinians will get to have their own state, and whether that state will be the home of Palestinian refugees displaced by the creation of Israel. The status of the city of Jerusalem, which is central to the faith of Christians, Muslims, and Jews, is another issue. There are also many questions of regional security, including the question of nuclear weapons, and the various issues between Lebanon, Syria, and Israel. One of these is Israel's occupation of Syria's Golan Heights, which it occupies not only for strategic reasons but also because it is the origin of the Jordan River and the Sea of Galilee, one of the few sources of water in the region. Water is a growing problem in the region because the only other sources of fresh-water are the Tigris and Euphrates rivers in Iraq. The region must find a way to share this scarce resource. The league is working on a solution that will meet the needs of its members and also accommodate Turkey. Perhaps once peace is made, these plans will also include Israel.

Another political objective of the league is to regularly present the positions of its members to the world, by rep-resenting Arab interests at the United Nations and in other world bodies. It also tries to resolve conflicts that flare up within member states and between its members, or between its members and nonmember states. In the last several years, the league has begun to work on the political conflict within Lebanon, and the one between Lebanon and Syria. The former is very complex because of the delicate balance between the country's competing religious groups, a situation made more dangerous by Syria's deep involvement in Lebanese politics and Israel's military incursions into the country. Both are related to the open conflict between Syria and Israel.

The league is also trying to find a solution to the genocide that is occurring in the Darfur region of Sudan, where since 2003 more than 400,000 people have been killed and another 2.5 million have been displaced. Somalia is another member state that the league is trying to help. It has not had a functioning government for almost two decades and has suffered from a terrible civil war and an invasion by Ethiopia. These conflicts have claimed about 400,000 lives and displaced another million in a population of only about 9 million.

This political assistance to African countries is part of a much larger and complex relationship between Arab and African nations. The league has always seen its regional interests as similar to those of other developing regions. Its members faced similar struggles to end Western colonialism and now they are all struggling to generate economic development. This sense of similarity is especially strong when it comes to Africa, because many league members are located on this continent. In the 1970s, the league directed some of its region's new oil wealth into institutions that would help Africa's economic development. These are the Arab Bank for Economic Development in Africa (BANDEA), and the Arab Fund for Technical Assistance to African and Arab Countries (AFTAAAC). Through economic assistance, the league hopes to help build up Africa, and in the process strengthen ties between African and Arab nations.

In June 2007, Arab League Secretary-General Amr Moussa (second from left) met with U.S. Secretary of State Condoleezza Rice and other foreign dignitaries to build a consensus on how to end the bloodshed in the Sudan's Darfur region. Initially, the Arab League rejected any military intervention or sanctions against the Arab militias in the Sudan, but as the situation worsened Arab countries pushed for a compromise, offering to dispatch a force of Arab and Muslim troops. The Sudanese government continues to hamper efforts to resolve the crisis.

The league also struggled to respond to U.S. involvement in the first Persian Gulf War, which occurred in February 1991, in response to the August 2, 1990 invasion of Kuwait by Iraq's leader Saddam Hussein. During this Gulf War the government of Saudi Arabia allowed a U.S. base to operate on its territory. This was a controversial decision because Islam's two most holy cities—Mecca and Medina—are in Saudi Arabia, and many league members feared that having a military base in the middle of the Arab world was the real motive for the war, leading to further Western domination. After the beginning of the 2003 Iraq war, people anticipated that it would undermine the stability of other countries in the region and bring old Sunni-Shi'a tensions to the surface, which is now happening.

WHAT ECONOMIC FUNCTIONS DOES THE ARAB LEAGUE PERFORM?

Modern states make rules about how the country's economy will run. States decide what kinds of businesses are legal and who can own them. States also set taxes, safety standards, and other regulations. They also decide whether and how goods and workers can move between countries.

In countries that have been colonized in the recent past, and are poor and lacking in many of the basic things needed to run a modern economy, one of the government's jobs is to encourage economic development, even though there typically is little money available to invest in new projects. The league has tried to tackle this problem by setting up organizations to assist its member governments and their business communities. Some of these organizations include the Inter-Arab Investment Guarantee Corporation, the Arab Fund for Economic and Social Development, and the Arab Monetary Fund. The latter helps its members develop their markets so businesses are more likely to invest in the country. It also helps to regulate foreign-exchange rates, which means it watches to make sure that one country's currency is accurately and fairly valued against another's. Finally, it helps with balance-of-payment problems that occur when one

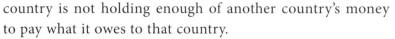

country is not holding enough of another country's money to pay what it owes to that country.

From its beginning, the league also established other institutions, programs, and regional policies to help states strengthen their economies, and to do so in ways that strengthen the region as a whole. In the league's early years, however, its members had conflicting ideas about how to pursue economic development, and this inhibited coordination. Some countries, such as Saudi Arabia and the small oil-rich sheikdoms located on the Persian Gulf, followed a more free-market capitalistic model of the economy, while others like Egypt, Libya, and Iraq under Saddam Hussein chose a mixed-market model in which the state does more to control the market. Therefore, early on, the league could only make serious progress by coordinating noncontroversial services such as telecommunications, postage, satellite communications, and broadcasting.

Even in these early years, however, the league did attempt more ambitious efforts. It formed an Economic and Social Council, and an Arab Development Bank (which is now called the Arab Financial Organization). In 1965, it set up an Arab Common Market to work toward getting rid of customs duties, and to help money and workers move freely between Arab countries. To encourage the Arab countries to link their economies, the league set up the Council of Arab Economic Unity. Then, to encourage good policies for producing and selling oil, it set up the Organization of Arab Petroleum Exporting Countries (OAPEC).

Very recently, as more of its members have adopted free-market policies, the league's efforts to expand intraregional free trade are beginning to meet with more success than when they first began to work on setting up a common market. Today they hope that as this continues to grow, they will be able to join the

World Trade Organization (WTO), which is the body that sets the rules of the global-trading system. For these reasons, the league established the Greater Arab Free Trade Area (GAFTA), which came into full effect in 2005. It brings together the league's 17 largest trading countries, which collectively have over 300 million consumers. This makes it one of the world's largest market spaces.

The History
of Colonialism
and the Rise of
Arab Nationalism

Colonialism, which is the direct rule of one country by another, was a very important force in the Arab world and played an important role in shaping the political ideas and institutions of the region. It influenced the development of Arab nationalism, the formation of the Arab League and the region's modern states, the relationships among Arab countries, and interactions between individual Arab countries and the outside world. The history of colonialism still deeply affects the region.

Between 1517 and 1922, the Middle East was ruled by the Ottoman Empire as a group of colonial provinces. The Ottoman Empire was governed from Istanbul, which today is the capital of Turkey. The *sultans* (kings) who ruled this empire were Turks and spoke Turkish. Starting in the second half of the nineteenth century, Europeans began to dominate the region and they continued to do so until the end of World War II.

Suffering from the effects of being ruled as colonies from afar, some Arab intellectuals (thinkers) and leaders began to

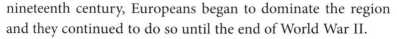

COLONIALISM

Colonialism is the annexation and direct rule of one country by another, done to satisfy the needs of the dominating country (for raw materials, a labor force, access to markets, a place for its "surplus population" or criminals, and/or national security). Colonies result when the government of one country takes control of other people's territory. A related form of domination is indirect rule. Between World War I and World War II (the closing era of European colonization), it is estimated that over 800 million people—one of every three people living at the time—were under the rule of a European country.

There are several types of colonies. Two of the most common forms are colonies of settlement and colonies of exploitation. In colonies of settlement, people from the dominating country settled permanently in the colony, often in order to establish small private farms. They typically excluded native inhabitants from their society and substituted their culture for an existing one or killed many inhabitants by violent measures or by exposure to disease. Examples of settlement colonies are Virginia (British colony), New Zealand (British colony), Algeria (French colony), and Quebec (French colony).

In colonies of exploitation, colonizers came as planters, administrators, merchants, or military officers, and lived alongside local inhabitants, which they used as a local labor force, often in large plantation agriculture devoted to producing crops for export

argue that all Arabic-speaking people (no matter what their religion) were part of the same nation and should be allowed to form their own independent state, just as European nations had done (e.g., France for the French, etc.). The idea that

such as cotton, coffee, sugar, rubber, and palm oil. In European exploitation colonies, Europeans established political control over the locals but did not displace native society or kill off the native population. Colonies of exploitation include Indonesia in Southeast Asia, and Nigeria and Ghana in West Africa.

Under indirect rule, a territory maintains its formal independence and local governing structures; however, the foreign power typically determines the territory's foreign policy and often those parts of the economy in which it has an interest (such as oil resources). By the early 1920s, all of the Arab world was divided into a patchwork of European colonies or was under indirect European rule. Some gained their independence peacefully, such as Bahrain and Kuwait, which were ruled indirectly. Others fought violently for their autonomy, which happened in the case with the French settler colony of Algeria. Bahrain, Qatar, and the states that make up the United Arab Emirates were the last to become independent, in 1971.

These historical relationships of domination and exploitation remain a key factor in the current underdevelopment of many countries commonly referred to as the "Third World," including many members of the Arab League. Memories of this experience remain an important part of the current political situation as well as an important source of Pan-Arab and Pan-Islamic identities. Today the term *neocolonialism* is used to describe how the West still dominates its former colonies by informal economic and political means.

each nation should have its own state is the core idea behind nationalism. The idea that Arabs should form one nation-state is the main idea behind Arab nationalism (also sometimes referred to as Pan-Arabism). Its goal is to unite all Arab-speaking people (the Arab nation) into one state.

Because it is not a religious ideology, Pan-Arabism also appealed to non-Muslim Arabs who were interested in fighting against Ottoman and European rule. In fact, many early leaders of the Pan-Arab movement were Christian Arabs who were attracted to this ideology rather than to Pan-Islam, which sought to unite all Muslims into one nation.

The ideas of Arab nationalism first began to take shape after Napoleon invaded Egypt in 1798. This is similar to the emergence of the idea that the American colonies should govern themselves, a reaction to British colonial rule, which led to the American Revolution in 1776. However, it was almost a century later, in 1875, in Beirut, Lebanon, that Pan-Arabism first became politically important, leading to oppositional political activities. It gained much more energy after a revolution in Turkey in 1908 strengthened the impact of Ottoman rule in the Arab world. This development led to the first Arab conference, a meeting held in Paris and attended by Arab thinkers, political parties, literary societies, and communities from Syria, Iraq, and Europe. At that event, Arabs did not call for Arab independence but only asked for governmental reforms and a decentralization of power within the empire.

A PLAN TO GAIN ARAB INDEPENDENCE

When the Ottomans became an ally of Germany during World War I, Arab demands changed because the Ottoman government arrested and tortured many Arab nationalists in Damascus and Beirut. It did this to ensure it would not face internal unrest while fighting the war. This treatment had the

In a series of letters known as the Hussein-McMahon Correspondence (1915–1916), British High Commissioner Henry McMahon promised Sharif Sayyid Hussein bin Ali *(front)* and his people the right to a new Arab nation in the lands of the former Ottoman Empire in exchange for help from Arab troops during World War I. With the signing of the agreement, Arab leaders worked with the British to capture many key cities. A year later, in 1917, Lord Arthur Balfour would offer the same land to the Jewish people.

opposite effect: it led Arab nationalist leaders to begin to call for Arab independence.

To achieve this goal they sought the support of the British, who were an enemy of the Ottomans. In an exchange of letters, known as the Hussein-McMahon Correspondence, Great Britain promised to support Arab independence after the war in exchange for Arab support for the British war effort. With the agreement signed, Arab leaders launched the Arab Revolt of 1916. This tied up Ottoman troops in the Arab region, which prevented them from attacking the British elsewhere. Working together, the Arabs and the British captured some key cities in 1917, and Damascus in 1918. Great Britain then conquered Palestine and Syria. Despite gaining this control, the British granted Arab independence to only a tiny territory. This is why most Arabs argue that Great Britain broke the promise they made in the Hussein-McMahon Correspondence.

After World War I, most Arabs still found themselves under colonial rule, so the goals of Arab nationalism continued to be independence from foreign rule and a demand for a truly sovereign and independent Arab nation-state. They made this case not only because Arabs had suffered much under colonialism but also because they believed a real Arab nation already existed, and just like the French or British nations, it deserved to have its own state. In other words, the Arabs just wanted the same thing that other people had. They argued that the boundaries of their Arab nation-state, logically, should coincide with the boundaries of where Arabs lived. Furthermore, one sovereign nation-state would also be practical because it would allow Arabs to set up institutions that would be strong enough to improve the harsh conditions in which most Arabs lived, which had been made worse by centuries of foreign and domestic exploitation. In summary, the goal of pan-Arabists was to create a new state that would replace the existing systems of exploitation with a new society based on the principles of justice and equality.[1]

A SECOND ATTEMPT TO ACHIEVE
FULL ARAB INDEPENDENCE

To achieve their pan-Arabist goals, Arabs needed institutions that would allow them to develop programs and policies to improve their societies. Between World War I and World War II, under conditions of only partial self-rule in some countries and continued colonization in others, Arabs created initiatives to achieve their dream of a fully independent nation-state. Practical steps taken in the 1930s in pursuit of that goal took the form of bilateral and multilateral treaties between individual Arab states and intergovernmental conferences to talk about developing common policies, and to make joint statements on important issues to outside powers.

A key event in this interwar period was the 1936 Palestine Revolt. This began as a protest aimed at ending Jewish immigration and land purchases in Palestine, which had increased after Hitler began implementing anti-Jewish policies in Germany that would later result in the Holocaust. Afraid they would become a minority in their own land, Arabs demanded that the British hold elections for a new government immediately, while they were still in the majority. The Arabs hoped that given their larger population, they would win such elections and would be able to form an Arab government. When the British refused this path, the Arabs revolted.

The methods of the revolt included not paying taxes, armed uprisings, bombing railroad tracks and an oil pipeline, and violent attacks on Jewish settlements. After some initial attempts to negotiate, the British cracked down on the revolt using 20,000 troops and unofficial assistance from Jewish paramilitary groups. At the end of the revolt in March 1939, thousands of Arabs, and hundreds of Jews and British were dead.[2] The other impact of the revolt was that it gave birth to Arab Palestinian identity, and Arab nationalists began to devote a lot of energy to the question of Palestine. They held two conferences, in 1937 and 1938, to discuss the issue.

THE LEAD-UP TO THE FORMATION
OF THE ARAB LEAGUE

In part as a response to the revolt, in 1939, the Great Britain held the London Round Table Conference with the governments of Egypt, Iraq, Jordan, Saudi Arabia, and Yemen. The purpose of the conference was to settle the future of Palestine. It resulted in Great Britain's issuing an official report stating it would not turn the territory into a Jewish state. Instead it sought to promote an independent Palestine in which Arabs and Jews would share authority in government. Great Britain further promised to allow only 75,000 more Jews to immigrate during five years, and all further immigration after that would require Arab consent. The British were again being attentive to Arab interests because by 1938 it was clear Great Britain was heading into another war with Germany, and it would again need Arab allies just as it had in World War I.

In 1941, as the Germans began to menace Arab lands under British influence, the British announced a new policy of support for Arab unity. British Foreign Minister Anthony Eden stated, "Many Arab thinkers desire for the Arab peoples a greater degree of unity than they now enjoy [and] . . . they hope for our support. No such appeal from our friends should go unanswered."[3] A few days later, when Germany invaded France, Great Britain supported Lebanese and Syrian claims of independence from France.

In February 1943, Eden repeated his pledge of British support for an organization to unify the Arabs. To this, Iraq's prime minister, and staunch British ally, Nuri al-Sa'id responded with a document known as the "Blue Book," in which he outlined a two-step plan to attain Arab unity.[4] First, a federation should be formed immediately among Syria, Lebanon, Jordan, and Palestine—with autonomy (independence and self-governance) for the Jews, and with Jerusalem as an international city. It should be put under the sponsorship of the United Nations (which was in the process of being formed). Second, the federation should be united with Iraq to form an "Arab league" that would have a rotating presidency and a council that represented each unit. This league would have responsibility for defense, foreign policy, currency control, communications, customs, education, and the protection of minority rights.

On March 6, 1944, Emir Abdullah of Jordan suggested a different plan for a "general Arab federation." At the same time, he demanded that he be made the ruler of "Greater Syria" (which was to be a union of Syria, Lebanon, and Jordan). This new state, he argued, could serve as a counterbalance to Iraq and Egypt, and as a real solution to the problems in Palestine.

THE CREATION OF THE ARAB LEAGUE

Although the proposals by Abdullah and al-Sa'id were opposed by Egypt, Saudi Arabia, and Syria, the ideas led to a meeting in September 1944 in Alexandria, Egypt, of the Preparatory Committee of the General Arab Conference. Leaders agreed to form a loose confederation of independent states, with a weak institution to coordinate some activities (similar to how the original 13 colonies were connected before the writing of the U.S. Constitution).

This document, the Alexandria Protocol, was an agreement to establish the League of Arab States. It stated that the signatories wanted to establish the league in order "to strengthen and consolidate the ties which bind all Arab countries and to direct them toward the welfare of the Arab world, to improve its conditions, insure its future, and realize its hopes and aspirations." It claimed to be doing this "in response to Arab public opinion in all Arab countries." More specifically, the signatories planned that the league should "coordinate their political plans so as to insure their cooperation, and project their independence and sovereignty against every aggression by suitable means; and to supervise in a general way the affairs and interests of the Arab countries."[5]

The protocol stated that in no case "will a resort to force to settle a dispute between any two member states . . . be allowed." Instead the league would have a council that "will intervene in every dispute which may lead to war between [member states] . . . so as to reconcile them."[6] Furthermore, the document expressed a hope that Arab states would be able to strengthen their ties, step by step, so as to create institutions which in the future would bind Arab states "more closely together." This was a nod toward the pan-Arabist goal of a unified nation-state.

Within days of signing the Alexandria Protocol, several heads of government who signed the document were removed. Mustafa al-Nahhas Pasha of Egypt was relieved as prime minister and denounced as a traitor. The prime ministers of Syria and Jordan were similarly dismissed. In Lebanon, the Alexandria Protocol was denounced as an attack on Lebanese sovereignty.[7] Clearly individual states were very concerned about losing their newly acquired power to the new institution, even though they did desire some type of organization to do regional coordination.

Still, over several months, a group met and wrote the charter for the League of Arab States. It took into account some of the objections that were raised against the Alexandria Protocol. On March 22, 1945, that committee transformed itself into the Pan-Arab Conference and signed the charter. This act formally established the League of Arab States. The charter does not mention the Alexandria Protocol, and it says much more about protecting the sovereignty of individual Arab states.[8] Specifically, while it does say the league's purpose is "the strengthening of the relations between the member state, [and] the coordination of their policies in order to achieve co-operation between them," the charter also says the purpose of the league is to "safeguard *their* [the member

During the formation of the Arab League, the main goal was the independence for all Arabs still under foreign rule. Today, the league is involved in political, cultural, economic, and social programs designed to promote the interests of member states. Saudi Arabian delegates El Zerekly *(right)* and Sheikh Youssek Yassin *(center)* are shown signing the charter on March 22, 1945.

states] independence and sovereignty; and a general concern with the affairs and interests of the Arab *countries.*[9] The charter also used some of Nuri al-Sa'id's original ideas, including the organization's name, the rotating chairmanship, a council that would represent each state, and the idea that the organization would oversee coordination of various areas of policy (excluding defense and foreign policy).

ARAB SOCIALISM: AN EXPRESSION OF NATIONALIST SENTIMENTS

Arabs sought independence to improve the lives of ordinary people. For many Arab leaders who were influential in the 1950s and 1960s, this meant that their commitment to Arab nationalism was also a commitment to embracing socialism. Therefore, Arab nationalism or Pan-Arabism is sometimes called Arab Socialism.

Those who believe in socialism argue that the state has a big role to play in running a country's economy. For example, one Arab Socialist idea is that the state should nationalize (own and/or control) the country's national resources. To Arabs this meant that Arab governments would be in charge of developing oil and other resources for the benefit of Arab people. This was better than having foreign governments and companies control these resources because they took the profits out of the country. Socialism also called for a fairer division of wealth, for giving small farmers access to land, and for ending poverty and hunger.

Arab nationalists also promoted the idea of "nonalignment" in foreign policy. This concept, which also is sometimes called "positive neutralism," holds that Arabs should not become close allies of any big, powerful country. This was a radical idea in the context of one of the harshest periods of the Cold War because during that time both the United States and the Soviet Union wanted other countries to become part of its "sphere of influence." Arabs argued that aligning themselves with either superpower would only increase tensions and make another world war more likely, and that war would be much worse than the last one because now both sides had nuclear weapons. Therefore, instead of siding with either country, Arab states should refuse to cooperate with each side's goals of increasing its power and instead take friendly assistance from both sides and keep their foreign policy neutral.[10]

Because Arab nationalism contained some socialist ideas, it was hard for Western countries to believe Arabs really meant what they said when they talked about positive neutralism and nonalignment. Because some Arab nationalist beliefs were also socialist, the West thought the Arabs and the Soviets must be working together against the interests of the West. While it is true that most Arab nationalists were skeptical about Western powers because of their experience with European colonization, most were friendly toward the United States. This is because in January 1918, near the end of World War I, President Woodrow Wilson, in his famous "Fourteen Points" speech, had implied that all people had a right to self-determination, and that the settlement of all colonial claims (including those of the British, French, and Ottomans) had to be done on the basis of the interests of the local people. Furthermore, Wilson said, in the future, all international agreements should be conducted in public. Never again should private deals like the ones that had led Great Britain to make conflicting promises to the Arabs, Jews, and French be allowed to happen. Arab leaders under-stood Wilson's speech to mean that the United States favored Arab independence from European colonization, an idea that made sense, given the United States also was a former colony of Great Britain.

The Arab's positive view of the United States was reinforced after World War II, when the United States recommended a two-state solution in Palestine that did a better job of protecting Palestinian interests than had the British plan. Unfortunately, the fear that the United States had of the socialism in Arab nationalism made U.S. policy makers engage in policies in the region that often ended up hurting the interests of states that were led by Arab Socialist leaders. This eventually caused a decline in popularity of the United States in the region.

These Cold War tensions were at their height in the first decades of the league's existence. They deeply affected the ability of the league to function because not all Arab countries embraced the socialist aspects of Arab nationalism, even though they all supported Arab independence. As a result of these political differences, and because the league had to make all decisions based on unanimous agreement, the league developed a habit of setting aside divisive and controversial issues. Over time this weakened the ability of the organization to take action.

Since the end of the Cold War, there are some signs the paralysis it caused might be ending. There has been real movement on the creation of a common market space within the region, and there also is more willingness to attempt to find solutions to conflicts that arise between league members, such as the secretary-general's efforts to resolve the conflict between Lebanon and Syria. However, it is also the case that since the end of the Cold War new issues have begun to divide the league. A major one concerned Iraq's 1990 invasion of Kuwait, followed by the United States' role in the first Gulf War a few months later. Even more contentious was the U.S. invasion of Iraq in 2003. This issue was so divisive the league was unable even to set a date to hold an emergency summit to discuss the issue. Bahrain, Qatar, and Kuwait were part of the U.S. war coalition, while other members completely opposed the war.

DIFFERENT WAYS TO THINK ABOUT ARAB UNITY

In the league's two founding documents, the Alexandria Protocol and the charter, as well as in earlier discussions about the nature of the future organization, different ideas were expressed about the meaning of the pan-Arabist dream of unifying all Arabs. In its earliest form, the vision was for a single unified state, in which all of the different existing governments would fuse into one entity and all Arabs would be citizens of one country. The approach taken by the league is different from that fusionist idea, and it reflects the real tensions that exist between the different interests of the existing Arab nation-states that are its members. The league exists today, and has always existed, amid these tensions. This has affected how it runs and likely will continue to do so into the foreseeable future. This is because the Arab world, just like most parts of the world, contains a variety of ethnic, racial, and religious minorities who face real problems of discrimination and oppression. This is a real problem in each of the league's 22 member states, and a problem that exists between Arab states. In addition, states have different levels of wealth and different allies outside the region, and hence they have different national interests. Each state also has its own political and economic elites who would lose power if one unified state were created. So these elites actively work to prevent any effort to increase the power of the league.

Nevertheless, it is still true today, just as it was during the colonial era, that there are issues and processes, both within the region and coming from outside, that can only be dealt with by creative regional solutions. This reality keeps the discussion about unity alive. In fact, these pressures may be growing today, for there is an increasing threat of Israeli military and economic domination in the region. Turkey and Iran also pose threats. In the case of Turkey these come in the form of its interest in Iraq's oil, its actions against its own Kurdish population, and future conflicts over increasingly scarce water resources. Arabs fear that Iran, a non-Arab, Shi'a, revolutionary society, seeks to dominate the Arab region and could destabilize conservative Sunni regimes. Another potential threat to the region is the growing economic leverage of the European Union and its efforts to form a Mediterranean trading bloc that only addresses European interests. Finally, since the Persian Gulf War of 1990–1991 there has been a strong U.S. military presence in the region that most Arabs see as hostile to their interests and aspirations. This is especially true since the beginning of the Iraq War and the War on Terrorism.

Other developments have occurred within the past few decades that also make some type of regional organization

Immigrant workers play a vital role in the economies of oil-rich states like Saudi Arabia, the United Arab Emirates, Oman, Qatar, Kuwait, and Bahrain. In some of these countries, temporary immigrant workers outnumber citizens by 2 to 1, and sometimes even 3 to 1. Here, two oil workers check an oil pump at the Kirkuk oil refinery northeast of Baghdad, Iraq, in 2002.

increasingly necessary. For one thing, there has been rapid growth in the cross-border movements of individuals who now frequently go from one state to another to vacation, shop, or visit. There are also a growing number of companies that operate in several Arab countries, as well as an increasing amount of cross-border investment, as oil-rich states look for new opportunities to make profits. Many poor people also move around in the region, as they go to oil-rich states in search of jobs, knowing that these states have small populations and so need more workers. All of this is facilitated by the growth of communications and transportation infrastructure that cross borders, and by the development of educational materials and systems that teach Arabs more about their whole region.

Increases in communications and flows of people, however, do not necessarily lead to a more unified political community. Strong national, religious, and ethnic identities prevent this, and new conflicts erupt as different groups come into closer and more sustained contact with one another. These are the new issues which now animate the older dream of regional integration and push it to take on new forms and expressions.

Arab states have now proved they can survive, so maybe in the future they will be more willing to cooperate, even as their continuing history as independent states makes their individual identities stronger. In some cases, Arab governments are becoming more participatory and representative in how they are governed. As this continues to happen, they may soon be capable of more coordination of joint policies with other states. This is most true in the area of economics, as countries move away from state-run economies toward more free-market models.

Today, there are many different ways to think about Arab unity, and this needs to be kept in mind as one thinks about how the region will integrate in the future and how the league continues to develop, both as an organizational structure and in terms of its economic and security policies. As one observer of the league has noted, if we mean by Arab nationalism "the fusionist" dream of the early days, then we should call the undertaker—for this project is dead. If, however, we mean an Arabism based on cooperation and coordination, which respects existing sovereignties, then we should call a midwife, because this type of integration is just being born.[11]

The Structure of the League of Arab States

ORGANIZATIONS ARE LIKE PEOPLE—THEY ARE BORN AND grow up slowly. Since its start, the league has grown in many ways. From its seven founding states (plus the stateless Palestinians who have a vote), the league has grown to 22 voting members, plus 6 nonvoting-observer members.

The addition of each additional member has an effect on all the others, for as more countries join, each pays a smaller share of the cost of running the organization. This also means each member has less influence, because the league must consider the interests and needs of more players. For instance, because of its size Egypt used to dominate the league, but in 1980 it was expelled for signing a bilateral peace agreement with Israel. Egypt was allowed to rejoin after about a decade, but now it has to work in a more cooperative way with oil-rich Persian Gulf states and other countries with large populations.

Other changes have also happened over the years, including the addition of new bodies, the use of new principles of operation, and changes in the way the league makes decisions. All three dimensions of change are evident in the creation, in 1950, of the league's Joint Defense Council. This body, which is discussed at length below, not only was an effort to expand the scope of Arab cooperation, it was another step in the league's commitment to the principle of mutual defense. Furthermore, decision making in the Defense Council does not require unanimous voting, as is the case in the League Council. This is because during its first 15 years of operation, the league learned that unanimous decision making meant decisions rarely got made. In 2005, after decades of good experience with the two-thirds rule in the Defense Council, the league's secretary-general proposed that the League Council also adopt the two-thirds rule to make the organization more efficient. This idea has not yet been adopted but it might be someday.

When the league formed on March 22, 1945, it was one of the only regional organizations in the world. Being one of the first, it had to invent ways of doing things. In the past 60 years, however, many other regional and international organizations have been created, and each has experimented with different ways of operating. Over time, organizations learn from one another and adopt ideas that work elsewhere. For instance, in 2005 the league created an Arab Parliament, which is an idea it borrowed from the European Union and the African Union. The league has also looked at other regions' common markets as it attempts to increase economic integration in the Arab region.

The United Nations (UN), which formed six months after the league, on October 24, 1945, has become a huge player in the international arena. As this happened, the league has developed a good relationship with the UN. The league sees the UN as setting global standards and often adopts its rules. The issue of Palestine is one area in which this is very evident. The league has repeatedly sought (and helped the Palestinians to get) UN recognition for issues affecting Palestine and to get UN resolutions passed on behalf of the Palestinians. The league has also undertaken joint ventures with UN agencies. It works with UNESCO on cultural preservation projects, and with UNICEF to encourage educational reform.

THE PURPOSE OF THE ARAB LEAGUE

The main idea behind the formation of the league was to work together to solve common problems within Arab societies and to help the Arab world grow strong and independent. From that broad vision the league set an ambitious agenda for itself that consists of many tasks:

- Promoting Arab security
- Supporting Palestine
- Helping Arabs gain their independence from Western colonialism
- Coordinating members' foreign policy
- Forbidding members to use force between themselves and helping to settle conflicts between members peacefully
- Generating economic and financial development and integration
- Developing agriculture and industry
- Developing communications and transportation
- Preserving culture and developing education
- Sorting out nationality issues (passports, visas, extradition of criminals)
- Advancing social affairs
- Promoting public health

At the same time as giving the league this ambitious agenda, the national leaders who created the organization set it up as a weak body. Not only does it not have a governing structure that is independent from the governments of its members, it also needs a unanimous vote in order to act. Since getting all states to agree is very difficult, often the league simply cannot act (which some leaders prefer).

Furthermore, as the league works, it has to walk a fine line between its Pan-Arabist vision and the reality of newly formed states who jealously guarded their new independence and do not want to give up much power to the league. There also has been a fierce struggle between the region's traditional leaders (kings) and newer types of rulers (democratic leaders and military dictators). The older and newer leaders have different ideas about how states should be run and how to develop their countries. These struggles make it difficult for the league to do its work. Adding to these tensions, until recently, were the politics of the Cold War which put pressure on states all over the world to get into line with the policies of either the Soviet Union or the United States. Since not all states in the region made the same choice in this regard, this too was a source of tension within the league. Since the first Gulf War in 1990–1991, intraregional security issues have also been a cause of division.

HOW THE ARAB LEAGUE IS ORGANIZED

Compared to many regional organizations, the size of the league's staff is small. In 1997, it had about 400 employees worldwide, and another 200 to 300 at its headquarters in Cairo, Egypt. In contrast, the European Union has more than 20,000 employees. Despite having a relatively small staff, the league has a complex structure with many specialized councils, permanent committees, specialized agencies, and other types of bodies.

The League Council

The League Council is the organization's supreme authority. It is the most powerful body and it makes all of the important decisions. It is composed of a representative from each member state, usually a foreign minister (a position that goes by the title secretary of state in the United States).

The council meets twice a year, in March and September, at the league's headquarters in Cairo. Extraordinary sessions can be called when requested by two or more members, or by the league's secretary-general (if approved by a third of the league's members). A member that has been attacked or threatened by another league member can also call a council meeting immediately.

In addition to the foreign ministers' meeting, each March there is a summit attended by the leaders of all the member countries. This meeting usually takes place at the league's headquarters or sometimes in a major city of the country which is presiding over the league at that time. Summits deal with all sorts of regional issues, and review the recommendations and reports submitted to them by the foreign ministers' meetings.

Each member of the league gets just one vote in the council, no matter how large its population. For all important matters, a unanimous vote is needed to make the decision binding. If only a majority approves something, it is binding only on the states that voted for the measure. A two-thirds majority vote is enough to make binding decisions on routine matters. Members who are fighting cannot participate in discussions and votes about their situation.

To get a sense of the diverse and complex issues that just one summit can cover, consider that the press report from the league's 2005 summit noted that the leaders had discussed, among other issues, the need to take joint action on issues linked to the Arab-Israeli conflict, the war in Iraq, Iran's occupation of three UAE islands, and how to get the United States to lift its

At a March 2007 meeting at its headquarters in Cairo, Egypt, Arab foreign ministers discussed Palestinian, Iraqi, Lebanese, and Syrian issues, as well as Israel's nuclear weapons.

sanctions on Syria. The summit also discussed improving Arab food security, increasing regional tourism, and examining the current status of the new Greater Arab Free Trade Area. Turning its attention to Africa, the leaders discussed the need to help bring peace to Sudan, to increase support to the government of Somalia and, in general, to improve Arab-African cooperation. It also discussed how to reform the UN and whether to send up an Arab satellite.[12] Of all these issues, as usual, the discussion about the Arab-Israeli conflict generated the most controversy; however, at this particular summit, Syria's presence in Lebanon was so divisive that it was simply not raised at all.

The council prepares reports and makes arrangements for summit meetings. Then it follows up to make sure that decisions made at summits are put into effect. It also writes policies and rules for running the league. The council has the power to amend the league's charter, to decide to admit new members and to accept the withdrawal of members (something Libya recently considered), and to expel members (as happened to Egypt). The council appoints the secretary-general and each year approves the league's budget. The League Council is also responsible for peacefully ending disputes between league members; defending any member that is a victim of aggression; and coordinating the league's work with other international organizations.

Special Permanent Committees of the League Council

The League Council is advised by special permanent committees. Each is made up of a small number of ministers from member states, plus some technical staff. These committees help the council implement the decisions made at summits. They also advise the League Council and its other bodies.

Specialized Ministerial Councils

Specialized ministerial councils are made up of the relevant government ministers from each member state. They formulate policies for the regulation and advancement of cooperation in their special area, whether that be housing issues, health, or the environment. For example, the Council of Arab Ministers for Youth and Sport meet periodically to promote issues that are important to children. They also coordinate the Pan-Arab Games which are discussed in Chapter 7.

Office of the Secretary-General

On a daily basis, the league is run by the Office of the Secretary-General (SG). It is made up of different departments, each headed by an assistant secretary-general. Although the SG and many staff people are located at the league's headquarters, it has staff all around the world.

The SG's job is to draw the attention of the League's Council and its member states to any problems that could hurt relationships between members, or relations with nonmember countries. The SG also makes sure that decisions made by the League Council are carried out. Initially the SG was not a powerful position; however, as the job has come to include representing the league in international forums and coordinating Arab positions on major international issues, the power of the office has grown. The SG also mediates disputes between Arab states.

The SG is selected by the League Council using a two-thirds majority vote for a five-year term, which can be renewed. The SG holds the rank of ambassador and has the right to attend all League Council meetings, including summits. The league has had six secretaries-general.

The current secretary general, Amr Moussa, is very popular. He is trying to reform the league to make it more effective.

SECRETARIES-GENERAL OF THE ARAB LEAGUE

NAME	NATIONALITY	APPOINTED	LEFT OFFICE
Abdul Rahman Hassan Azzam	Egyptian	1945	1952
Abdul Khlek Hassouna	Egyptian	1952	1972
Mahmoud Riad	Egyptian	1972	1979
Chedli Klibi	Tunisian	1979	1990
Dr. Ahmad Esmat Abd al-Meguid	Egyptian	1991	2001
Amr Moussa	Egyptian	2001	present

AMR MOUSSA, SECRETARY-GENERAL

The current secretary-general, Amr Moussa, was born in 1936 and studied law in Cairo. In 1958, after completing his education, he started his career in the Foreign Ministry of Egypt, and became ambassador to India in 1967. In 1990, he became Egypt's UN ambassador. A year later he was made Egypt's foreign minister. He earned a reputation for being a tough critic of Israel and of U.S. policy in the Middle East.

Moussa was made the league's secretary-general in May 2001, and was re-elected in 2006. Critics of Egyptian president Hosni Mubarak say he got Moussa elected to get him out of the way. It

might not have worked. Not only has he been featured in a hit song by Egyptian singer Shaaban Abdel Rahim, but tens of thousands of people signed an online petition asking Moussa to run for president of Egypt in 2005. In 2006, during a TV interview, he was asked if he had presidential hopes. The 72-year-old Moussa responded by saying only that he hoped to continue the successes that had occurred under his leadership at the Arab League.

Main Departments Under the Secretary-General

A big part of the SG's job is to oversee the departments that are under this office, each of which is also overseen by an assistant secretary-general. Each department writes reports, and develops and carries out projects that are in line with the policy goals established by the League Council. Departments cover the issues that are most important to the league's regional responsibilities (as is the case with the Departments of Economic Affairs, Military Affairs, and Palestine Affairs). There also are departments devoted to the league's international operations, as is the case for the Department for Administrative and Financial Affairs.

Arab Parliament

The newest part of the Arab League is the Arab Parliament, which was established in 2005. Its members are drawn from the parliaments of member countries. Each state has four representatives, bringing the Parliament to a total of 88 seats. It meets twice a year and is located in Syria.

The Parliament's scope of activity extends only to social, economic, and cultural issues. It cannot propose new legislation, and can only discuss and give opinions on matters that are referred to it by the League Council. Even with this limited power, the body has already made its voice heard. At its second-ever meeting, in 2006, it asked Ethiopia to withdraw its troops from Somalia. It also requested the UN Security Council to end all foreign presence in Somalia.

Many Arab citizens think the Parliament will be valuable only if it monitors Arab governments. This will be hard for it to do because it has no legislative (law-making) power. The European Parliament, however, was not powerful when it started, but over time it has grown in importance. Many hope the same will happen with the Arab Parliament, and that someday citizens will be able to elect its members and that it will then be allowed to write laws.

OTHER SPECIALIZED ARAB ORGANIZATIONS AFFILIATED WITH THE ARAB LEAGUE

The Arab League has 26 specialized organizations to take care of specific functions related to Arab integration. They have grown over time in response to different needs. The Arab Labor Organization in Cairo works to standardize laws about work across the region; to promote good working conditions for labor; and to provide technical assistance. It also helps to resolve labor disputes. The Arab Satellite Communications Organization in Riyadh, Saudi Arabia, operates five satellites and works to develop regional satellite telecommunications systems for television and telephones. The Arab Organization for Agricultural Development in Khartoum, Sudan, facilitates cooperation in agriculture and specializes in research and training aimed at food security and water management. These are reported in its various publications.[13]

ARAB UNIONS

Arab unions bring together companies and other types of organizations from different countries to coordinate actions across the region that are helpful to their members. These include groups such as the Arab Sea Ports Federation, the Arab Association of Iron and Steel, and the Arab Postal Union.

LEAGUE MISSIONS AROUND THE WORLD

The league has a presence in many countries around the world with offices known as "missions." These are similar to the embassies of nations in that they work to represent the interest of the league to the governments of the countries in which they are located. In Africa, the league mission is in Nairobi, Kenya. The league also has missions in the world's two most populated countries, India (in New Delhi) and China (in Beijing). Its European missions are in Berlin, Brussels, Geneva, London, Madrid, Moscow, Paris, Rome, and Vienna. There is one South American mission in Brazil, and in the

Government leaders have promoted women to prominent positions based on merit and qualifications. Nancy Bakir, a former deputy secretary-general for social affairs of the Arab League, was selected by Prime Minister-designate Nader Dahabi to the post of Culture Minister of Jordan. He also added three other women to ministerial posts in Jordan.

United States there is the league's UN mission in New York City that concentrates on issues that come before the UN. It also has a regular mission in Washington, D.C. that focuses on dialogue with the U.S. government.

WOMEN AND THE LEAGUE

Despite the fact that some conservative Arab countries, like Saudi Arabia, do not like women and men to work together, the league hires a lot of women. Since Amr Moussa has been the secretary-general, the promotion of women to higher levels has been a priority. Currently there is one female assistant secretary-general who heads one of the divisions of the secretary-general's office. Women head several other bodies, including some overseas missions. In recent years, the Arab League has added a department to focus on women's issues. It also works with other organizations to host conferences that address the special issues women face.

The Arab League and Israel

MORE THAN ANY OTHER ISSUE, THE CONFLICT BETWEEN ARAB states and Israel has been at the center of the league's work and even behind its formation. This is also the issue over which the league is most often judged, and on which it has done the most consistent work. This issue is key to determining relationships between Arabs and the rest of the world: it has influenced the league's approach to security and how it interacts with Africa, Asia, and the UN. Since 1948, the league has helped to create a leadership structure for Palestinians (Arabs from Palestine) who became stateless people after the formation of Israel.

Arabs' experience with colonialism taught them they must stand together in order not to be dominated. In the twentieth century, while the situation in Palestine was changing quickly,

Arabs united to demand that Palestine become part of an independent Arab state. Arabs also opposed Jewish immigration into the area and protested the taking of Arab land. European powers that controlled the region largely ignored these protests. Later, Great Britain went back on promises it made to Arabs in 1915 when it needed their help during World War I. For Arabs, the formation of the state of Israel is linked to Great Britain's double-dealings and is seen as a moral wrong and an affront to their sovereignty and self-determination.

The Palestinians' struggle has placed a heavy burden on Arab countries, for since 1948 they have had to assist hundreds of thousands of Palestinian refugees who even today live in refugee camps in Lebanon, Syria, and Jordan. In 2007, more than 3.7 million Palestinians were listed as refugees with the UN, and more than 1.2 million of them still live in camps. This situation is often referred to as the "Palestinian problem," and it has several dimensions. First, some believe if Arab states permanently resettle this refugee population, Israel is rewarded for not coming to terms with the Palestinians, making it likely that more Palestinians will suffer the same fate. Second, historically Arab states have been underdeveloped and they still frequently suffer from high rates of unemployment, so it has been difficult for them to commit fully to integrating Palestinians permanently into their countries.

Third, Palestinian refugees are seen as a source of political instability. Their experience has made them impatient with the existing political situation and eager for change. They desire not only a change within Israel/Palestine but also democracy and good government elsewhere in the Arab world. This makes kings and military rulers distrustful of them. This view has been reinforced by the fact that frustrated refugees have formed military organizations wherever they live and from these locations have launched military strikes against Israel. In its turn, Israel has developed a policy of retaliation: it conducts air strikes and other campaigns on countries from which Palestinians conduct any violence against Israel. This obviously puts Arab states in a difficult position, increasing their nervousness about hosting refugees, and further expanding the dimensions of the Arab-Israeli conflict.

HISTORY OF AN ANCIENT LAND

Today when people make claims about "Israel/Palestine," "Israel and the Occupied Territories," or the Middle East in general, they often refer to events that happened long ago.

Initially this area was called Canaan and was occupied by the Canaanites who had lived there for 1,500 years before the Jews (Israelites) arrived in the twelfth century B.C. Palestinians are assumed to be descended from the Canaanites and other people who arrived later. Since ancient times, this territory has been called both Israel and Palestine.

The establishment of the Kingdom of Israel dates from about 1000 B.C. Solomon, one of Israel's first kings, built the First Temple to Yahweh (Hebrew for God) in Israel's capital, Jerusalem. Between 722 and 539 B.C., many Jews were forcibly resettled in Mesopotamia by the Assyrian and Babylonian empires. After the Persian Empire defeated the Babylonians in 539 B.C., they allowed Jews to return. It was at this time that the Jews built the Second Temple on the same location as the first.

Eventually the territory came under Roman rule, and, in A.D. 66, a Jewish group known as the Zealots rebelled. To punish them, the Romans destroyed Jerusalem, including the temple. Today, all that remains of that structure is its western "Wailing Wall." When the Roman Empire began to decline in the third century, it imposed harsh taxes that led many Jews to leave the area again. Jews were no more than 8 percent of Palestine's population after that. This began to change in the 1870s, when European Jews began to arrive, animated by Zionism, which is the name for Jewish nationalism. This was occurring around the same time as Arab nationalism was emerging.

PALESTINE UNDER ISLAMIC RULE

Islam came to this region in the middle of the seventh century and to Jerusalem in 638. Many local people converted to the new religion, and, in 691, the Muslims built the Dome of the Rock, a mosque that is Islam's third holiest site. Located on the site of the former Jewish temple (of which only the Wailing Wall remains), Muslims believe this is the place where the Prophet Muhammad ascended to heaven.

Western Crusaders conquered Jerusalem in 1099, killing thousands of Muslims, Jews, and Christians. Jerusalem became a Christian city in which no Jew or Muslim could worship or live. In 1187, Muslims recaptured the city, and from 1250, Palestine was ruled by various Muslim regimes, the last of which was the Ottoman Empire. It took control in 1516 and ruled until the end of World War I.

THE RELEVANCE OF WORLD WAR I
TO THE REGION TODAY

In the period leading up to World War I, and during the war itself, the British and French maneuvered in this region in support of their war efforts and what they thought their interests would be after the war. Because the Ottomans sided with the Germans in World War I, the British encouraged Arabs in the Ottoman Empire to rebel, in order to weaken the Ottomans' ability to fight them in Europe. Meanwhile, Great Britain was also trying to strengthen its alliances within Europe and with the United States, for in the early years of the war it looked like Germany might win. This led the British to make a series of conflicting promises to different groups; those promises still haunt the region today.

In an exchange of letters between Great Britain's high commissioner in Egypt, Sir Henry McMahon, and Sharif Hussein of Mecca, between July 1915 and March 1916, the British seemed to support Arab independence after the war—if the Arabs would fight with them against the Ottomans. The language McMahon used in his letters was ambiguous, so it was unclear whether Great Britain promised that Palestine would be included in a future independent Arab state. Hussein understood that it would be included, and, on that basis, he declared war on the Ottomans in June 1916. The Arabs were successful in their fight and expected Great Britain to keep its promises. After the war, however, the borders of the independent Arab state—including Palestine—became a point of bitter debate. Arabs maintain Palestine was to be included, but Great Britain has insisted that this was not the case.

While the British were negotiating with Hussein, they were also negotiating with France and Russia, their allies against the Germans. These partners signed three secret agreements in 1915. According to the Sykes-Picot Agreement, Palestine, because of its holy places, was to become an international territory, while territory to its northeast was to go to France, and the southern part to Great Britain. Thus, the same land that Arabs believed had been promised to them in March 1916 had already been divided up differently a month earlier in this secret European agreement!

In addition, Great Britain also negotiated with the leaders of the Zionist movement (Jewish nationalists who were fighting to establish a Jewish state in Palestine) because it feared Russia might withdraw from the war after the Communist revolution of 1917. This would have allowed the Germans to concentrate all their forces against France and Great Britain. Great Britain thought that if Zionists believed it supported their goals, Russian Jews would convince the new Russian government to stay in the war. Great Britain also believed that supporting Zionism would lead American Jews to encourage President Woodrow Wilson to enter the war on Great Britain's side. On November 2, 1917, British Foreign Secretary James Arthur Balfour sent a letter to Lord Rothschild, a major British Zionist leader, declaring British sympathy for Zionist goals. Called the Balfour Declaration, it stated that the British government "views with favour the establishment in Palestine of a national home for the Jewish people, and will use its best endeavours to facilitate the achievement of this object. . ."[14]

PALESTINE UNDER THE BRITISH MANDATE (1922–1948)

When the war ended, the League of Nations, a newly created international body, set up a mandate system to govern territories formerly ruled by the Ottomans and the Germans. Under this system, territories were to be governed temporarily by the winners of World War I, who were to rule in a way that prepared the territories to become independent countries. Arab lands were considered ready for independence if they took advice from a mandate power. The determination of which country would be a territory's mandate ruler was to be made after considering the wishes of local peoples. In this part of the world, that was determined by a U.S. commission sent to the region to talk to local people. It concluded that one Arab state should be formed with the United States as the mandate power, but this did not happen. Instead, the French took over Syria and Lebanon and the British got Iraq and Palestine.

The British then created a new territory out of part of Palestine and called it Trans-Jordan (which today is usually written Transjordan or simply Jordan). They hoped that splitting Palestine in this way would decrease Palestinian nationalism and thereby pave the way for them to keep their promise to help create a Jewish homeland in Palestine.

These policies angered Palestinians and Zionists. Arabs argued the Hussein-McMahon Correspondence had pledged the land to them. Zionists argued Palestine had been promised to them in the Balfour Declaration.[15] For the next 25 years, the British were unable to resolve the situation. Instead, things only got worse, as each side tried to take matters into its own hands. The Zionists did this by organizing a well-structured government and by depending upon the British for support.

The Arabs rejected all British-run, Arab-Zionist governing bodies, for to have joined them would have been to accept the legitimacy of the Balfour Declaration.

After 1923, Palestinian communities became isolated, as Zionists refused to lease or sell land to Arabs, or to hire them. Adding to the Palestinians' problems was the fact that in 1930 only about 25 percent of Palestinian men could read, as compared to 90 percent of Jewish men.[16] Rising Jewish immigration was another factor. Between 1922 to 1936, the Jewish percentage of the population grew from 10 percent to 27 percent.[17]

Because of Jewish immigration and its impact on land ownership in the territory which was changing in the context of a major global economic downturn (known as the Great Depression) and rising religious tensions, Palestine became the scene of violent fighting between Arabs and Jews. In 1929, a riot broke out that led to the deaths of 472 Jews and 268 Arabs. After that, the British issued a statement saying that despite a report issued by their own government recommending Great Britain end Jewish immigration, it would not do so. Arabs refer to this document as the "black letter." After it was issued, they regarded Great Britain as their enemy. Zionists also did not like the letter, for it seemed Great Britain was not really committed to their goal of creating an independent Jewish homeland in Palestine.

Immigration became a more urgent problem after the Nazis came to power in Germany in 1933; the Nazis immediately began implementing anti-Jewish legislation, starting with banning Jews from civil service jobs. In 1935, Jews were forbidden to join the military, had their citizenship rights withdrawn, and racial purity laws were put in place that banned marriage between Jews and non-Jews. The next year Jews were banned from professional jobs. Anti-Jewish activity came to a head on November 9, 1938, in the *Kristallnacht* (the Night of Broken Glass) during which Jewish businesses were vandalized, synagogues burned, about 90 Jews were killed and at least 20,000

The Arab Revolt in Palestine (1936–1939) was driven primarily by hostility to the British mandate allowing restricted Jewish immigration and land purchases in Palestine. Palestinian Arabs believed that this would lead to their becoming a minority in the territory. Here, British soldiers escort a group of Arab prisoners from the Old City of Jerusalem on October 26, 1938.

arrested.[18] This is usually considered to be the beginning of the Holocaust that killed 6 million Jews.

Between 1929 and 1939, a period which Jews call the Fifth Aliyah (ascent), about 400,000 Jews came into Palestine, bringing the total Jewish population to 450,000 by 1940. At that time the Arab population was about a million.[19] In 1936, Arab anger at immigration erupted into the Arab Revolt. The Great Britain sent 20,000 troops to stop the fighting. Its Peel Commission issued another report calling for the partition of Palestine into Jewish and Arab sections. Both sides rejected the plan and fighting resumed. In 1939, the British announced that after five years, Jewish immigration would be stopped, and within 10 years a united Palestine would receive a constitution that would guarantee Arab representation and protect Arab land rights. At that point, Jews began to launch terrorist attacks on the British.

THE FORMATION OF ISRAEL

At the end of World War II, the United States led the effort to set up the United Nations, which replaced the League of Nations. Just as the League of Nations at the end of World War I had been given the task of deciding what to do with the former colonies of the losers of that war, the UN was given the job of deciding what to do with Palestine when Great Britain announced, in September 1947, that it planned to leave the territory. The UN set up a special committee that recommended Palestine be divided into two independent states, one for Arabs and one for Jews, with Jerusalem as a neutral territory under international administration. This UN Partition Plan was approved by a 33-to-13 vote in the UN's General Assembly on November 29, 1947. While Jews largely accepted the proposal, Arabs opposed it.

At the beginning of May 1948, the British began to withdraw and on May 14 the Zionists declared Israel had been formed. The next day President Truman surprisingly became the first to recognize the new state. The Soviet Union immediately followed suit. Also on May 15, the member countries of the Arab League attacked Israel and the league's secretary-general said they would destroy the new state. Despite harsh statements, the Arab states did not coordinate their efforts. After a month, the 1948 Arab-Israeli War ended with Israel in control of 21 percent more land than it had been given in the UN's Partition Plan. It now controlled about 80 percent of Palestine. The Arabs were defeated and more than 650,000 Palestinians became refugees.[20]

This military defeat had a huge impact on the Arab world, as Arabs asked "why did we lose Palestine?" After much soul-searching, they answered this question in the following ways: First, Arabs had been too naïve, believing that they would prevail because their cause was just. Second, effective lobbying by Zionists (and sympathy for Jews because of the Holocaust) had swung world opinion to the Jewish side. Third, the West financed and armed the Zionists, while Arabs had not taken care to arm themselves properly. Fourth, and most importantly, Arab society was "sick and defective."[21] This last answer meant old traditions and systems within Arab countries needed to be replaced, which began to happen as Arabs took out their anger at the military defeat on their own governments. Three coups d'etat occurred in Syria between 1949 and 1950. King Abdullah of Jordan was assassinated in 1951. The same anger produced the Free Officer's Revolution in Egypt in 1952, and the Algerian Revolution in 1954. These changes brought a new generation of radical leadership into power that was eager to transform their countries using a vision that combined Arab nationalism with socialism. This ideology is often called Arab Socialism.

THE PALESTINIAN QUESTION AND THE FORMATION OF THE ARAB LEAGUE

Part of the logic and energy needed to form the Arab League had been generated by Arab efforts to gain independence in Palestine. Thus it is not surprising that in the 1944 Alexandria Protocol, the first document that led to the formation of the league, there is a statement of strong support for the Palestinians. In fact, about a third of the document is devoted to this issue. Then the 1945 League Pact document, which formally established the league, created a seat on its council for a representative from Palestine. That same year, the league set up the Arab Higher Committee as a governing body for Palestinians, followed a year later by the Arab Higher Executive. Neither body worked, so in 1948 the league created the

All-Palestine Government. Though this body was recognized by all league members except Jordan, it did not capture the imagination of many Palestinians.

In the 1950s, Palestinians developed their own organization called *Al-Fatah* (Arabic for "opening"), which took ideas from Algerians who were liberating their country from France by using urban terrorist tactics. When Al-Fatah began to use these tactics against Israel, Israel responded with military air strikes on the countries hosting Al-Fatah fighters. This made Arab countries nervous about hosting Palestinian refugees.

Given that Al-Fatah was so popular, but dangerous to the interests of Arab states, in 1959 the league decided to get control of the situation by creating another new Palestine government, the Palestine Liberation Organization (PLO). In 1964, the league proclaimed the PLO was the first official representative of Palestine since 1948. At the same time, however, the league made it clear that all resolutions passed by the PLO had to be ratified by the League Council. In this way, the league tried to make sure the PLO acted in the interests of the league and its other members.[22] In return for this control, the league financed PLO operations and supported the Palestinian delegation at the UN.[23]

The league had to decide whether the PLO—as a government, even though in exile—should have its own army. Instead of allowing the PLO to have a separate military organization like Al-Fatah, the league decided Arab states should establish Palestine units in their national armies; Palestinian refugees could also join the league's new Joint Arab Command. Rather than solving the problem, however, this policy created a situation in which each country supported its own Palestinian organization. Thus by the late 1960s, there were about a dozen armed Palestinian groups.

Yassir Arafat, a founding leader of Al-Fatah, became head of the PLO in 1969 and began to unite these armed groups. He was so successful that in 1973, various Arab states reaffirmed that the PLO led by Arafat was the *only* legitimate representative of the Palestinian people. This was important because it opened the way for Arafat to address the UN in 1974. After that, the UN General Assembly passed several resolutions declaring the right of the Palestinians to seek independence. It also granted the PLO permanent observer status, which usually is the step before full membership. In this way, the PLO gained full international legitimacy, but it was still not recognized by Israel so it could not directly negotiate with it (even though by 1975 the PLO hinted it would accept the existence of Israel if Palestinians were granted their own country in the West Bank and Gaza).

THE ARAB LEAGUE BOYCOTT OF ISRAEL

In addition to setting up the PLO and taking military action against Israel, the league set up an economic boycott of Israel. This boycott covered the trade of all Jewish products and manufactured goods to Arab countries. All Arabs were asked "to refuse to deal in, distribute, or consume Zionist products or manufactured goods."[24] The boycott had three layers. The "primary boycott" covered all products and services that had their origin in Israel. The "secondary boycott" concerned all businesses that operated in Israel. The "tertiary boycott" dealt with businesses that had relationships with other businesses that operated in Israel. The league also took action to prevent other organizations (such as the Afro-Asian Conference) from recognizing the state of Israel, and it encouraged non-Arab states to participate in the boycott.[25] Each member state had its own boycott office, which was advised by the league's central boycott office.

Until the late 1970s, the boycott was enforced and observed by all members of the league. As a result, products such as Coca-Cola were not found in the Arab world (because they refused to participate in the boycott). The opposite was true of Pepsi and McDonald's, which supported the boycott and so did not sell their products in Israel.[26]

How effective was the boycott? At its height, more than 8,000 companies were not allowed to trade with the Arab world. In 1957, when Air France invested in Israel, the league announced its members would deny the airline the right to fly over or land in their countries. After 18 months, the airline changed its policies. At one point, the Israeli Chamber of Commerce estimated Israel's exports and foreign investment were 10 percent lower than they would have been without the boycott. It was not lowered by more than this because often Israeli goods are shipped through a middle country, often Cyprus, ending up in Arab markets.[27]

Since 2005, only Lebanon and Syria still strictly impose the boycott. Egypt was the first to abandon it, in 1980, followed by Jordan and the Palestinian Authority in 1995. More recently, the countries in the Gulf Cooperation Council have decided to enforce only the primary boycott. Bahrain and Saudi Arabia ended their participation in 2005 in order to get in line with the requirements of the World Trade Organization and U.S. law.

In addition to running the boycott, the league refused to cooperate with Israel on any regional efforts, boycotting meetings attended by Israel, demanding implementation of UN resolutions, and lobbying the UN to change Israel's boundaries back to the borders before the 1967 War. In 1977, the UN's General Assembly created the "International Day of Solidarity with the Palestinian People," which is observed on November 29.

MILITARY RESPONSES

Since the 1948 Arab-Israeli war, Arabs and Israelis have engaged in many rounds of fighting. In between, relations have remained hostile.

In 1950, all of the league's members signed the Joint Defense and Economic Cooperation Treaty Between the States of the Arab League. Although the JDEC does not mention Israel by name, it was a response to the establishment of Israel and to the Arab defeat in the 1948 war. On the basis of the JDEC, the league set up a number of security bodies. The main one was the Joint Defense Council (JDC).

In October 1956, Israel and the West became worried about Egypt for several reasons, including the growth of Pan-Arabism under Gamal Abdel Nasser, Egypt's drift toward the Soviet Union in the Cold War, and its nationalization of the Suez Canal and move to deny Israelis use of the canal or the Straits of Tirana. In response, Israel, Great Britain, and France invaded Egypt and in four days gained control of the Sinai and Gaza. The United States and the Soviet Union, however, opposed this development, and after a few days the invading forces left and UN troops were stationed on the Egyptian-Israeli border in Gaza and Sinai.

NASSER: A NEW KIND OF ARAB LEADER

Gamal Abdel Nasser (Jamal 'Abd al-Nasir) is one of the most important figures in recent Arab history. A symbol of Arab dignity, he had a huge following in the Arab World in the 1950s and 1960s.

Born on January 15, 1918, this postman's son got interested in politics at age 11 when he participated in a political demonstration against the British. At that event, he was hit in the face with a police baton and put in jail. After Egypt was defeated in the 1948 Arab-Israeli war, he led the Free Officers who overthrew King Farouk, in 1952. This event was celebrated by ordinary people who were hungry for change and hoped the new government would improve their lives.

(continues)

(continued)

In 1956, Nasser became president, a job he held until his death in 1970. He stood for Arab freedom and unity, and sought to foster development in Arab countries. Nasser became so popular that people talked about "Nasserism" when discussing Pan-Arabism, and Egypt became the center of the Arab world. Nasserist clubs and political parties formed in many countries, inspiring

a coup in Libya in 1969 and producing the short-lived United Arab Republic (1958–1961). Nasser outlined his philosophy in a 1959 book, *The Philosophy of Revolution.* Guided by these ideas, he organized a land reform, which limited the amount of land any family could own and gave land to poor people. He nationalized large industrial, mining, financial, and commercial companies. The state invested in electricity, constructing huge dams, the most famous of which was the Aswan Dam that required a worldwide effort to move ancient temples. Nasser also created a modern system of free education and pushed the Arab League to develop a collective security pact because he believed real Arab unity was cooperation in the face of danger.

Nasser's reputation declined after he lost the 1967 Six-Day War, and because he used repressive measures to deal with political opponents. His legacy is still hotly debated in the Arab world. To many, he is a great reformer. To others he led Egypt into grave defeats and was too repressive.

Although Israel had won a military victory, Nasser scored a political victory. He was hailed as the leader of the Arab world and Pan-Arabism became more popular.[28] It was at this time that Nasser encouraged the league to strengthen its security arrangements. This resulted in the establishment of a Joint Arab Command, which since 1964 has had a large budget and a permanent planning staff. It is supposed to make the Arab world ready for another major attack.

After the "Suez Crisis," Israel began to develop nuclear weapons. It also began diverting 70 percent of the Jordan River's water for its own use. This greatly upset Syria so it permitted Al-Fatah to use its territory to launch raids into Israel.

In May 1967, Arab leaders became convinced Israel was about to attack Syria, so Nasser marched his troops through Cairo on their way to the Suez Canal. He told the UN to withdraw its troops and announced that the Straits of Tirana were again closed to Israeli ships. On June 5, the Israeli air force attacked, destroying Egypt's air force while it was still on the ground. Within a week, Israel had taken the Sinai and Gaza from Egypt, the West Bank from Jordan, and the Golan Heights from Syria. Since then, Gaza and the West Bank have been called the Occupied Territories. The status of this land is still a very controversial issue today.

In response to this 1967 Six-Day War, the UN Security Council adopted Resolution 242 requiring that Israel withdraw its forces from the Occupied Territories and that Arab states recognize Israel's right to exist. To date, UN Resolution 242 has not been implemented. Israel continues to occupy all the land it gained in 1967 (except the Sinai, which was returned to Egypt in 1980 in exchange for peace and formal recognition).

The 1967 Six-Day War completely changed the situation in the region. The military defeat was the end of Nasser's power and of the broad popularity of Pan-Arabism. The situation also changed in dangerous ways for Israel, for it now occupied territory in which more than a million Arabs lived. This has greatly boosted Palestinian identity because now instead of being ruled by other Arab states, a majority of Palestinians are ruled by Israel. It also fuels anti-Israeli activity, which in turn creates a security problem for Arab host countries. This led the king of Jordan to attack Palestinian refugees in 1973. When many of them fled to camps in Lebanon and began to attack Israel from there, it invaded Lebanon in 1982. For these reasons, the league endorses the Palestinian demand that they be allowed to exercise self-determination in a state of their own and that all refugees be allowed to return to Palestine.

In 1973, Syria and Egypt attacked Israel in the Yom Kippur War. They did this in an effort to improve their weak bargaining position. The strategy worked. The United States got involved, which eventually led to a peace deal between Egypt and Israel in 1979. Egypt got the Sinai back in return for recognizing Israel's right to exist.

The conflict between Syria and Israel has not been resolved, and it remains a major issue within the overall Arab-Israeli conflict. At the heart of the issue is the Golan Heights, which Israel does not want to return to Syria because it is high ground from which attacks can be launched, and more importantly because this is the major source of the water used by Israel.

LIFE IN THE TERRITORIES TODAY

The PLO's leadership was driven out of Lebanon by an Israeli invasion in 1982 that resulted in the massacre of many refugees. The PLO's exile to Tunisia left Palestinians living in the Occupied Territories without any political direction. The next year, after the center-right Likud party came to power, Israel began to adopt harsher policies toward the Palestinians and greatly expanded the expropriation of Arab land and increased the development of Israeli settlements.

This happened in the context of an economic downturn. As a result, the Palestinians' situation became more difficult. This led to the First *Intifada* (Arabic for "shaking off") in

The sealing up and demolishing of the homes the Israeli government says are connected to Islamic militants has been a controversial subject within the international community and within Israel as well. Several activist organizations against the bulldozing assert that often entire neighborhoods are razed, leaving innocent and underprivileged civilians virtually destitute.

1987, which was an uprising of ordinary people in Gaza and the West Bank that lasted until the Oslo Accords in 1993. This spontaneous and unplanned event was quickly organized and sustained through a series of local neighborhood committees that restricted the protest to mass demonstrations and stone-throwing. Knives and guns were banned in order not to negatively affect world opinion.[29]

Israel saw the intifada as a dangerous new phase of the Palestinians' struggle for an independent state that threatened to harm core interests and destabilize Israel. To restore order, the Israeli government responded with a military plan called "Iron Fist." This consisted of putting Palestinians in jail for many months without formal charges, collective punishment such as bulldozing the homes of the families of alleged participants in the intifada, large-scale deportation of Palestinians, and the further denial and removal of Palestinian land rights. These policies are very controversial internationally, and within Israel as well, because according to the Geneva Conventions and other international treaties, land conquered during war is subject to the international laws of war and to international humanitarian law. This humanitarian law includes the special protection of individuals in those territories, limitations on how conquered land can be used, and the granting of access to international relief agencies.

Responding to their people's actions, the PLO's leadership in 1988 declared Palestine an independent state[30] (as the Zionists had done decades earlier). Given nervousness over Israeli government policies during the intifada, many countries in the international community received this announcement happily, and the United States reopened official discussions with the Palestinians after a 13-year block. In September 1993, the PLO and Israel granted each other mutual recognition during the Oslo Accords, which were signed at the White House, though as of 2008 this peace process has not ended the conflict. The following year Jordan signed a peace agreement with Israel and then in March 2002, the league offered Israel full recognition and the establishment of normal relations in exchange for a return to the pre-1967 borders, the acceptance of a Palestinian state in the Occupied Territories with East Jerusalem as its capital, and a just solution to the refugee problem. Israel's response was that as an initial signal, demonstrating a new willingness to negotiate with Israel could be a positive development but that its particular pieces were not acceptable.[31] As of 2008, this proposal has gone no further. Out of step with the rest of the league, Syria and Lebanon (which is greatly influenced by Syria) still reject peace with Israel.

Despite these steps forward in the official peace process, life has not improved for people living in the Occupied Territories.

As a result, even though the PLO has renounced terrorism, young men (and sometimes women) still engage in suicide bombings and other violent acts. In fact, many young people, especially in Gaza, have turned away from the PLO to support the more radical and Islamist organization *Hamas*, which was created in 1987. It has neither renounced terrorism nor accepted Israel's right to exist (although in 2007 they did discuss a cease-fire). For these reasons, levels of violence between Israel and the Occupied Territories increased again after 2000 and some now call this situation the Second Intifada.

In 2005, Israel officially withdrew from Gaza; however, it still controls access into the territory and strictly limits the ability of people and goods to come and go. Israel argues it must do so for security reasons, because Hamas, as of the beginning of 2008, was launching rockets into Israel. In late 2007, the UN's Relief and Works Agency warned that if more access to Gaza was not granted, the situation could become a humanitarian crisis.[32]

Another very controversial issue is the construction of a huge barrier, which the Israelis call a "security fence," that when finished will run 436 miles and completely enclose the West Bank. To Palestinians, it is an "apartheid wall." The Israeli government says it is building the wall to prevent terrorist attacks, but the placement of this barrier also gives Israel more land. Palestinians are being squeezed into a completely controlled space, on less and less land. Water and other desirable resources are often placed on the Israeli side, and the Palestinians' ability to earn a living is compromised since Israel controls the few armed gates that lead to the outside world. In addition, a series of highways have been created throughout the West Bank that can only be used by Israelis to move between their settlements. The situation is a powder keg.

Sixty years after the creation of Israel, the world is still trying to find a way to deal with the conflict in this territory. In the heyday of Arab nationalism, Gamal Abdel Nasser argued that Arab unity "is the road to Palestine." Palestinians have long argued that Nasser's statement is wrong. Instead, they say, "Palestine is the road to unity."[33] By this they mean that if the Palestinian problem gets settled, many tensions in the league will go away, and then it will become a stronger voice promoting common Arab goals. At present, a solution to this conflict appears to be a long way off, and after the terrorist attacks on the United States on September 11, 2001, the league began to turn away from the Palestinian issue. Shortly after that event, the league made strong statements against terrorism, and it is now focusing more on the problems created by the U.S. invasion of Iraq, by the growing influence of Iran, and by the problems of violence in Somalia and Sudan. It is also paying attention to the secretary-general's efforts to focus the league on economic issues and other problems.

5

Economics in the Arab World

FOR MANY HUNDREDS OF YEARS, THE ARAB WORLD WAS AN
economic space linked by trade routes. This was highly developed under the Roman Empire, which set up a network of
roads because the area was its major supplier of food. The
Romans called Egypt their "breadbasket."

After the Roman-era, roads deteriorated and camel cara-
vans were used to move goods within the region, and to
connect the region to Europe and to China and India. It was
because the Arabs had such a lock on interregional trade
that the Portuguese and Spanish searched for an alterna-
tive sea route to the Far East. This led the Portuguese to go
around the southern tip of Africa, and the Spanish to invest in
Christopher Columbus's trip across the Atlantic in 1492. These

voyages began the age of European colonization that became worldwide—and also deeply affected the Arab world.

After about 1850, private European companies began to invest in the Arab world. They signed special contracts with local governments called "concessions." A concession gave a company monopoly (sole) rights to develop and run part of a country's economy. It was not uncommon for a European company to be given a monopoly concession to develop all of a country's railroads or all its telegraph lines. Such deals were often so large that they affected a country's whole economy, and sometimes even its politics.

Through such arrangements, the Arab world was drawn into the global economy in new ways that sometimes had negative effects at the local level. Egypt is a good example. Cotton was a major product at the beginning of the Industrial Revolution, which began in Great Britain around the 1830s. At first, Great Britain got raw cotton from India, but after about a decade it began buying mostly from the United States, where it could get a type of cotton that worked better in the new mechanized weaving looms. U.S. cotton was also cheaper because it was grown using slave labor. During the American Civil War (1861–1865), the North blockaded the South, preventing it from selling its cotton. Seeing this possible threat, Great Britain and France invested heavily in cotton growing in Egypt. When the war ended, however, those nations quickly returned to using U.S. cotton, and this hurt the Egyptian economy.

During this same period, a French company was granted a concession to build the Suez Canal. This canal links the Mediterranean Ocean to the Red Sea, making it possible to transport goods from Asia to Europe without having to go around the southern tip of Africa. Work on the canal began in 1858 using forced laborers (like slaves). It took longer to build than expected because forced labor became a controversial issue. Not only was the American Civil War being fought over this issue, but Great Britain made loud criticism of it, even

In the nineteenth century, Egypt began to specialize in growing cotton, and it still commands over one-third of the world market for long-staple and extra long-staple cotton. Advances in technology have allowed textile mills of nearly comparable quality to be built for less than half the cost. Farmers cannot earn enough to cover costs and have switched to growing other cash crops.

though just a few years earlier it had used forced labor to build Egypt's railroads as part of its investment in cotton. The reason Great Britain made forced labor an issue is because it was worried that once the canal was built, other European powers would get access to India, its richest colony.

The canal opened in 1869 but, due in part to the controversy over forced labor, it cost twice as much to build as expected. This left the Egyptian government with a huge debt it could not pay. This, combined with the loss of cotton sales after the U.S. Civil War ended, caused the Egyptian economy to fall apart. Great Britain took over the country in 1882 and ruled it officially until 1922 (and unofficially until Egypt's revolution in 1952).

Another major development that deeply affected the region's economy was the mass production of cars, which began in Germany in 1902. With cars, petroleum became an important resource. European powers tried to control the economies of oil-rich countries, especially Saudi Arabia, Iraq, Iran, Kuwait, and the little states along the Persian Gulf.

European investment in the Arab world had two other important effects. The first is that during the colonial era, each Arab country got closely connected to a European economy. At the time of independence, colonial trading relationships were formalized in bilateral treaties between former colonizer and colonized: France in the case of Lebanon, Syria, Algeria, Morocco, and Tunisia; Great Britain in the case of Egypt, Iraq, Jordan, and Sudan.[34] So even at the beginning of the twenty-first century two Arab countries located next to each other trade more with Europeans (and the United States) than with other league members. This situation is exacerbated by the fact that most countries in the region export the same commodities (petroleum and its by-products, chemicals, raw cotton, textiles) and desire to import the same items that are not produced in the region (heavy machinery, cars, foodstuffs). In other words, rather than having economies that are "complementary," in that they each produce different commodities, economies in the Arab world are "duplicative." This is one of the issues the league has attempted to address while it has worked on increasing regional economic integration.

European colonialism also had a lasting effect on agriculture. Large-scale European investments (e.g. cotton, in the case of Egypt) reinforced feudal relationships. Under feudalism, one powerful rich person controls huge amounts of land, which is worked by many poor peasants. This pattern of production creates societies that are divided between a few rich people and huge numbers of poor farm workers who own nothing, have no education, or any independent way to earn a living. This was the situation many Arab countries faced when they became independent.

ECONOMIC DEVELOPMENT AND
THE POLITICS OF THE COLD WAR

Countries ruled by traditional monarchs (kings) are often supported by the rich landlord class. So such governments did not try to change the structure of their economic systems very much. They also tended to rely on, for the most part, the mechanism of the free market in which individual firms decide what and how to produce.

In contrast, in states that became republics after independence, or were controlled by military dictators whose goal was to transform the division of wealth and/or modernize their countries, the government tried to change the feudal system using state-led development projects that grew out of the ideas of Arab socialism. This meant they usually set up mixed economic systems. Just as in free market systems, in mixed-market economies most decisions about consumer goods are made by private companies, guided by consumer demand. The difference is that the state owns or controls important industries (such as steel, energy, and telecommunications) and national resources (oil, the Suez Canal, etc.).

States use this control to regulate the economy. For example, the government might set the prices for basic foods so they are affordable for poorer workers. This is one way governments try to maintain political stability and remain in power. Or the state may decide what can be imported and exported (which it does to make sure the country uses its foreign currency wisely). Governments in many of these countries must make difficult choices among development projects because there is not enough money to do all the things the country needs.

Historically, many Arab governments ran mixed economies. This certainly was true for those countries committed to Arab socialism. It also was true for some of the more conservative countries as well, for two reasons. First, the experience with the negative effects of the use of concessions under colonialism, described above, taught all countries in the region that it was not a good idea to allow foreigners to have complete ownership of key parts of the economy, or of key national resources. Second, due to the lack of development and the absence of private groups with enough money to make large investments, the state was often the only entity that could generate enough resources to build key infrastructure (e.g. water treatment plants, phone systems, etc.) and develop key industries (e.g. petrochemicals).

This economic development was happening during the Cold War, so both the United States and the USSR made their views about development strategies known. Many Arab leaders tried to maintain a "nonaligned" foreign policy during the Cold War, not siding with either the United States or the USSR. When Arab countries pursued domestic policies that were influenced by Arab socialism, or even just nationalism, Western countries thought they were siding with the USSR and so put a lot of pressure on such states.

The superpowers also maneuvered behind the scenes at the league to line states up to support their side in the Cold War. These tensions created by the Cold War hurt the ability of the league to work on economic development. So even though the league, from its beginning, had ideas about how to develop the region and set up many organizations to implement those ideas, in its early years it was not very successful. Not much economic development or regional integration occurred until the 1970s. Then new political and economic events related to oil opened up new possibilities for economic development in the Arab world.

OIL WEALTH AND THE SECOND WAVE OF ECONOMIC DEVELOPMENT

Since the eighth century, Arabs have used petroleum to tar roads and later to light city streets. What made oil such an important export, however, was the widespread adoption, around the beginning of the twentieth century, of the internal combustion engine used in automobiles and other moving vehicles. From then on, oil became a major export commodity. In the last third of the twentieth century, natural gas also became important. The Middle East and North Africa (MENA) region has the largest known reserves of petroleum and natural gas, and for many decades these have been its the most important exports and source of money for development.

Only a few of the league's members have large oil and gas deposits: Algeria, Iraq, Libya, and the oil sheikdoms along the Persian Gulf (Bahrain, Dubai, Kuwait, Oman, Qatar, Saudi Arabia, and the United Arab Emirates). The latter group of countries account for about 45 percent of the world's proven oil reserves and 25 percent of its oil exports. Saudi Arabia is the world's largest oil exporter and has at least 17 percent of the proven global natural gas reserves. Qatar is the world's fourth-largest exporter of liquefied natural gas. Oil contributes about a third of the GDP in these countries, and between 46 percent (UAE) and 92 percent (Kuwait) of exports between 1999 and 2002. Furthermore, oil financed between 53 percent (UAE) and 76 percent (Oman) of all government spending in those years.[35]

This unequal division of oil began to have a huge impact on the MENA region after the price of oil tripled in the 1970s. A key part of that story has to do with the actions of the Organization of Arab Petroleum Exporting Countries (OAPEC). OAPEC was formed in 1967. It is located in Kuwait, and since about 1990 it has had ten functioning members: Algeria, Bahrain, Egypt, Iraq, Kuwait, Libya, Qatar, Saudi Arabia, Syria, and the UAE. OAPEC works to develop the region's oil industry and on other projects designed to increase regional integration. In these efforts, it often cooperates with the league, including by helping to fund the Arab Monetary Fund. It also helps to set up and sponsor new companies, such as the Arab Detergent Chemicals Company and the Arab Drilling and Workover Company. It provides training in technical matters and publishes reports on the oil industry.

On October 17, 1973, members of OAPEC announced they would no longer ship oil to nations that had supported Israel in its conflict with Syria and Egypt. This was also an opportunity to use their leverage to renegotiate contracts with the Seven Sisters (the seven oil companies that dominated mid-twentieth-century oil production and distribution). The effects of the energy crisis were felt worldwide as the increase in the price of oil led to both global inflation and an economic recession.

In 1973, during the Yom Kippur War, when Egypt and Syria attacked Israel, OAPEC and the Middle Eastern members of the Organization of the Petroleum Exporting Countries (OPEC), including Iran (not an Arab country or member of the Arab League), decided to cut oil production by 5 percent a month until all Israeli forces left the Occupied Territories, which Israel had controlled since the 1967 Six-Day War. The embargo lasted five months and only ended when the United States got involved.

This oil embargo taught OPEC they could make political gains by manipulating the amount of oil they produced. They used this new power to renegotiate contracts with the world's oil companies, so that Arab oil-producing countries could keep a larger share of the profits. These are the reasons oil prices rose so much in the 1970s.

Overnight, countries with oil became fantastically rich. They used their new wealth to begin huge development projects that required much labor to build. Between 1973 and 1983, about 4 million Arabs from poor countries went to work in the rich oil states, sending back almost $4 billion a year to their families.[36] Today this no longer is the case because most of these building projects were completed in the 1990s. After the 1991 Persian Gulf War, migrant workers were kicked out of Kuwait for political reasons. They also are increasingly unwelcome elsewhere, not only because the building of large infrastructure projects has largely been completed, but also because the countries that used to employ a lot of migrant workers now face new challenges. These countries have experienced high population growth in the last 20 years, and large numbers of women have entered their labor markets. These factors have put much pressure on these countries to create new jobs at a pace of more than 4 percent a year. This is likely to continue because about one-third to one-half of their populations is under the age of 15. Another increasing barrier to labor migration is that countries now have development programs and institutions devoted to educating and training their own citizens, in an effort to make them ready for the jobs of the future.[37]

In addition to workers sending back money to their families, oil money also flowed through the region from rich to poor Arab countries in the form of aid. Between 1976 and 1989, about $5.1 billion a year was given.[38] Most of this money was channeled through the Islamic Development Bank (IDB) and the OPEC Fund for International Development (OFID). Some money flowed through the league-run Arab Fund for

Economic and Social Development (AFESD) and the Arab Monetary Fund (AMF). Rich oil producers in the region also made money available to Arab states through the World Bank and the International Monetary Fund (IMF). Altogether, this aid was equal to about 14.5 percent of the money generated by Arab oil exports in 1987. This was about 3.5 percent of the GDP of the donor countries as a group, which is a lot, especially when it is compared to the amount of aid given by rich Western countries to poor countries, which typically is less than 0.5 percent of their GDP.[39]

TERMS TO EXPLAIN THE ECONOMIES OF THE ARAB WORLD TODAY

There are many ways to talk about an economic system. Some of the ways an economy can be looked at include the amount of wealth it generates, the type of goods and services it produces, or the type of relationship that exists between the government and economic actors.

Level of Income

The World Bank divides countries into four categories based on how much wealth they generate each year. Low-income countries are those in which most people earn less than $905 a year. Another way to say this is that the country has a per-capita (per-person) income of less than $905 a year.[40] This means that many people in these countries live on less than $3 a day. The Comoros, Mauritania, Somalia, Sudan, and Yemen are the league's low-income members. They have annual per-capita incomes of about $650. There is a subcategory of extremely low-income countries in which people live on less than $1 a day. Eritrea is the only league participant at such a low level, with a per-capita income of $170 a year! Like other countries that suffer from such extreme poverty, Eritrea's economy is heavily based on subsistence agriculture (growing food for direct consumption), it suffers from periodic droughts, and is recovering from over 30 years of war (which it fought to gain independence from Ethiopia). The Arab region has a lower percentage of people living in extreme poverty than any other region of the world.

The income of lower-middle-income countries ranges from $906 to $3,595 per person annually. Nine league members (if the Occupied Territories are included) are in this category. At the low end of this range is Djibouti at $1,060. At the high end is Algeria, at $3,030.

In upper-middle-income countries, people earn between $3,596 and $11,115 per year. Libya, Lebanon, and Oman fall into this category. The oil-producing kingdoms of Bahrain, Kuwait, Saudi Arabia, the UAE, and Qatar are extremely high-income countries, with the wealthiest, Kuwait, at $30,630. For comparison, consider that the per capita income of the United States, which ranks fourth in the world, was $44,970 in 2007.

In 2002, the United Nations Development Program released a special report on the Arab world. It showed that in the 20 years before 2000, the per-capita income of Arabs had grown by 0.5 percent a year, which was the second-slowest rate of growth in the world. During that time, between 15 percent and 30 percent of people across the region were unemployed, with younger workers suffering even higher unemployment rates. Despite slow economic growth during this period, other measures of human development, such as education, life expectancy, and health all improved dramatically. Between 1980 and 2000, the adult literacy rate almost doubled, and women's literacy rate tripled. Life expectancy increased by 15 years, and the number of children who died before their fifth birthday fell by two-thirds. These improvements likely were the result of development programs and government policies that specifically targeted these issues.

Since 2000, the price of oil has again risen dramatically, and this has helped Arab economies to grow faster (at a rate of 6.2 percent in 2006). Many argue this growth rate is also linked to the fact that since the mid-1980s Arab states have slowly begun to move toward less government regulation of the economy and toward more open markets. One indication that economic reforms are having an effect is that in the first five years of the twenty-first century, the amount of foreign direct investment (a measure of how much money foreigners were willing to invest), grew in the region, from $5.9 billion in 1999 to $24.4 billion in 2006. Whatever the causes, the fast growth rate brought regional unemployment down to 10.8 percent by 2005, though it is still much higher in some countries. This growth has also led to a large decrease in the rate of poverty.

The Nature of Work

Many low-income countries have agricultural economies in which the majority of workers grow food or harvest other natural products, such as cotton or rubber. Typically, middle-income countries have industrial economies. This means at least half of all workers manufacture goods. High-income countries often are postindustrial, a term that means a major-ity of workers are employed in providing services to other people (teaching, selling insurance), creating knowledge (doing research, writing books), or processing information (computer programming).

The league's six agricultural economies fit the pattern of being low- or lower-middle-income countries. The league's high-income countries are split between the industrial and postindustrial categories, with the common element being that they all get most of their wealth from exporting oil.

Promoting Economic Development and Regional Integration

ONE OF THE THINGS MODERN STATES DO IS MAKE RULES ABOUT how the economy of the country will run—what kinds of businesses are legal or illegal, who can own companies, how companies are organized, what kind of safety measures employers must put in place, and what sorts of taxes must be paid on economic activities (wages or profits). They also decide whether and how goods and workers can move between countries.

In countries that have been colonized in the recent past, many of which are poor and lack many of the basic things needed to run a modern economy, one of the government's jobs is to encourage economic development even though there typically is little money available to invest. The Arab League has tried to tackle this problem of a lack of funds by setting up a series of lending organizations.

Given its Pan-Arabist vision of promoting Arab unity, the league also sought to promote economic development by promoting greater regional economic integration. Regional integration is the process of increasing cross-border economic linkages in trade and investment, as well as, for example, roads, power lines, and educational curriculum.

The league's initial years of operation coincided with an era of radical change in many Arab countries, as revolutionary regimes challenged traditional socio-economic systems, such as feudalism, using government power to impose economic reform through state control of key sectors of the economy. This also was the heyday of the Cold War. For both reasons, in its early years the league's members had conflicting ideas about how to promote economic development. Some countries embraced a capitalistic market economic model while others opted for a mixed economy that entails more state control. As a result, the league's earliest successes in integration were limited to coordinating noncontroversial services such as telecommunications, postage, satellite communications, and broadcasting.

It is only since the end of the Cold War that a consensus has formed about the need to try more market-based approaches. This, in turn, has made real strides toward integration possible for the first time in the Arab world. They are also more possible at the beginning of the twenty-first century because in the past 60 years populations have grown and economies have diversified. League countries now have more that 300 million consumers, and a combined gross domestic product of $1,148 billion (in 2006). By these statistical measures, the Middle East and North Africa is similar to Southeast Asia and South America, regions whose regional organizations, which are the Association of Southeast Asian Nations (ASEAN) and the Southern Common Market (Spanish: Mercado Común del Sur, or MERCOSUR) respectively, have achieved higher levels of economic integration than MENA.

In 2002, the Gitex technology exhibition in Dubai attracted vendors and buyers from around the world and is one of the largest of its kind. Dubai has a booming economy due to tourism and hosting trade shows, and is quickly developing into a hub for service industries like information technology and finance.

LEAGUE BODIES THAT WORK ON ECONOMIC DEVELOPMENT AND INTEGRATION

The first body the league set up to work on economic development and integration was the Economic and Financial Committee (EFC). It advised the league on how to promote scientific research, teach modern farming methods, set up agricultural cooperatives, invest in transportation, standardize statistics, and create a regional banking and currency system. The economic department in the Office of the Secretary-General was another body that was established at the beginning. Its job was to survey the economic conditions in Arab countries and prepare statistics.

In 1950, the league got more power to work on economic issues from the Joint Defense and Economic Cooperation Treaty

(JDEC). One of the region's most important treaties, the JDEC, gives the league a plan for working on economic and security issues. With respect to economics, the JDEC commanded the league to set up ways to provide for "welfare and development" in Arab countries by promoting cooperation and coordination.

To work on these goals, the league set up the Arab Economic and Social Council (AESC) in 1953. The members of AESC are the economic ministers of member states. It makes decisions by majority votes, which are final; they do not need to be approved by the League Council (which requires unanimity and thus often cannot act).[41] The work of the AESC is to: (1) coordinate the economic policies of member states; (2) oversee the league's economic development and integration work; and (3) supervise all of the league's specialized economic bodies. In this work it calls upon all of the league's other economic bodies.

In 1959, the league set up the Arab Development Bank (now called the Arab Financial Organization), and in 1965, it set up an Arab common market to work toward abolishing customs duties, facilitating the free movement of capital and labor, and coordinating the economic development policies of member states. It also set up the Council of Arab Economic Unity, which also tries to integrate the region economically. Another important coordinating body, discussed in the last chapter, is OAPEC. OAPEC coordinates policies around the production and sale of oil.

THREE WAVES OF REGIONAL INTEGRATION EFFORTS

In the decades before the 1970s, the league promoted regional integration by pursuing three strategies simultaneously. First, it drafted several conventions, or treaties. One stipulated a new set of trade rules that allowed participants not to pay customs duties (taxes) on raw materials and things made from agricultural products (e.g., clothing from cotton). Another convention made it easier to move money between Arab countries for the purposes of investment and trade.

One problem with these early treaties is that they lacked enforcement mechanisms, so they never had much effect on region-wide trade. However they did become the basis upon which many bilateral trade agreements (between just two countries) were made, and this did increase local trade between individual countries.

The second way the league pushed integration was by establishing new organizations that promoted various forms of economic development. For example, the Arab Development Bank encourages joint projects between different countries by providing loans, loan guarantees, and technical studies. It resulted in the creation of new firms, such as the Arab Tanker Company and the Arab Pipeline Company.

A third way the league tried to integrate the region was by setting up a region-wide common market. The idea was that by standardizing trade rules and regulations, and lowering tariffs (taxes on trade) and other trade barriers it could create a market space among countries that resembled a market inside a single country in which it is easy to do business. The initial attempt to create an Arab common market occurred in the early 1960s, first among Jordan, Egypt, Iraq, and Syria. Later, Kuwait, Libya, Mauritania, Palestine, Somalia, Sudan, and Yemen joined. The Arab Common Market (also called the Common Arab Economic Union, or CAEU), was modeled after the European Common Market that eventually became the European Union (EU). It allowed for the free movement of money, goods, and labor. Although the CAEU was an important step, it did not work very well because in that era barriers to trade could not be undone simply by signing treaties.

JOINT ARAB ECONOMIC ACTION: THE STRATEGY OF THE SECOND WAVE

Twenty years later, a more ambitious attempt to encourage regional trade was made. As noted previously, during the 1970s the price of oil tripled, and as a result the oil-producing Persian Gulf states became very rich. In 1980, with new money and confidence, the league launched a second wave of economic integration. It was called the Strategy for Joint Arab Economic Action (JAEA). The JAEA consisted of 26 agreements and created several new organizations, including the Arab Authority for Agricultural Investment and Development, to lend money to new businesses, and the Arab Institution for the Insurance of Investments, to provide insurance to new companies.

The new General Union of Arab Chambers of Commerce, Industry and Agriculture for the Arab Countries also helped promote integration. This is a federation of individual countries' chambers of commerce that helps companies lobby governments and regional organizations to create policies and laws that are favorable to business. Integration was also promoted by more than 250 "joint companies" formed either between two companies from different countries, by two or more Arab governments, or by a combination of a government and a private company. Another 269 projects and companies combined an Arab company or government with a non-Arab company.

The most important part of the JAEA was the establishment of three subregional trading blocks (rather than the older regional market, the CAEU). There is a big debate about them because some think they weaken the league, while others believe they help to implement its goals.

COOPERATION COUNCIL OF THE ARAB STATES OF THE GULF (GCC)

The first to form, in 1981, the Gulf Cooperation Council, or GCC, is the most powerful and successful of the three subregional organizations. Its members are the wealthy oil states of Bahrain, Kuwait, Oman, Qatar, Saudi Arabia, and the UAE. In 1983, it approved a Unified Economic Agreement to achieve "equal economic citizenship" for all people living in GCC countries by giving them the legal freedom to start a business and export goods to other GCC countries. The agreement

At the fifth consultative meeting of the Gulf Cooperation Council in Riyadh, Saudi Arabia, the GCC leaders stand for a group photo beneath the organization's logo. The Persian Gulf countries have some of the fastest-growing economies in the world, mostly due to oil and natural gas revenues. Although Iran and Iraq are on the Persian Gulf, they are excluded. Yemen has applied for membership and hopes to join by 2016.

also has provisions for linking these countries' infrastructure networks (i.e., roads, electrical lines, etc.) and for standardizing the functioning of seaports, investment mechanisms, laws, procedures and measures, quarantine rules, record keeping, and the use of pesticides, fertilizers, and medicine. Its most ambitious goals are to coordinate its members' economic policies in agriculture and industry, and when possible, to set up joint projects. The agreement also encourages individual GCC governments to take a common stand on international issues, especially trade agreements and the bulk purchasing of basic commodities.[42]

Despite rich members, ambitious goals, and more than 20 years of development, intraregional trade within the GCC still only amounts to about 4.5 percent of total trade (which is mainly oil to countries outside the region).[43] That is very different than the situation among the NAFTA countries of the United States, Mexico, and Canada. Regional trade among them accounts for 70 percent of their exports.[44]

UNION OF THE ARAB MAGHREB (UAM)

The UAM formed in 1989 and is headquartered in Rabat, Morocco. The idea for this union first surfaced in 1956 when Tunisia and Morocco gained independence. Nothing happened until 1986, when Algeria, Libya, Mauritania, Morocco, and Tunisia held a summit meeting at which they agreed to set up the UAM with a rotating chairmanship. Even after its formation, the UAM was stymied by the long rivalry between Morocco and Algeria over the efforts of the Western Sahara to get free from Moroccan interference. As recently as 2005, a summit was canceled when Morocco refused to meet after Algeria had voiced support for Saharan independence. The level of economic integration achieved by the UAM is minimal, with only 2.6 percent of total exports accounted for by trade within the union.

ARAB COOPERATION COUNCIL (ACC)

The ACC was formed in 1989 by Iraq, Jordan, Egypt, and North Yemen, in part because they were left out of the Gulf Cooperation Council. This organization fell apart before it ever really got off the ground, due to Iraq's invasion of Kuwait a year later. After the invasion, all further meetings were canceled. In 1994, Egypt officially ended its membership in the moribund organization. Even without the war, it is unlikely the organization would have thrived because its members did not share many common interests.

WAS JOINT ARAB ECONOMIC ACTION SUCCESSFUL?

Economic integration in the Arab League has been successful only in some sectors. In the late 1990s, intraregional trade still amounted to only about 6 percent of all Arab trade, which is the same percentage as before the project started.[45] One reason for this is that most countries in the region produce the same goods; the economies duplicate one another so there is not much reason to trade. In addition, many of the region's consumers still prefer exports from outside the region for reasons of quality and cost.

Transportation facilities within the region are under-developed, and it is expensive to get goods across this wide market area. This is changing, in part due to the efforts of the Arab Maghreb Union that is working with the United Nations Economic Commission for Africa (UNECA), the African Development Bank (ADB), and the African Union to complete a 5,366-mile (8,636-kilometer) highway that follows a sea route along Africa's Mediterranean coast. Known as Trans-African Highway 1, it will run between Cairo and Dakar (Senegal) when completed in 2010.

Other issues which impede further integration include growing religious and ethnic conflict within and between countries, continued division between countries due to their external alliances, and tensions between rich and poor Arab states. Also slowing integration are political elites who understand that real economic integration will eventually lead to more political integration, and greater demands for democracy and human rights. If granted these will undermine their own power.

Despite such problems, there are some bright spots. In the past 25 years Lebanon, Syria, and Jordan have linked their electricity networks, reducing seasonal shortages and surpluses. Agricultural trade has increased in the region and this has reduced the amount of food imported from outside to 15 percent of all imports. Still, half of all food eaten in the region comes from overseas. This is a source of food insecurity.[46]

THE THIRD WAVE: GAFTA AND ECONOMIC INTEGRATION

Between 2001 and 2006, the price of oil tripled, and the price rise is again stimulating economic integration. The result is that league members have again moved to create another region-wide common market initiative called the Greater Arab Free Trade Agreement (GAFTA). This time other global forces are also pushing in the same direction.

GAFTA was a long time in the making. It started with the signing of a treaty in 1981, which began to get implemented in 1997, when 17 league members signed a second agreement that established GAFTA. These countries were: Egypt, the United Arab Emirates, Bahrain, Jordan, Tunisia, Saudi Arabia, Sudan, Syria, Iraq, Oman, Palestine, Qatar, Kuwait, Lebanon, Libya, Morocco, and Yemen. In 2006, Algeria applied for membership and has been in the process of finalizing procedures to join as the 18th member.[47]

GAFTA allows for the sharing of databases, information services, and standards. Most importantly, it created a timetable to eliminate all customs duties between members, and it succeeded in doing this in 2005. GAFTA is already working better than JAEA or the original CAEU. In May 2006, Egypt announced that since GAFTA began, its pan-Arab trade had increased by 40 percent.[48] Similarly, that year Jordan said that GAFTA countries account for 42.6 percent of its exports and 36.1 percent of its imports.[49]

Helping GAFTA to succeed is the fact that since the mid-1980s many league states have begun to move toward a more free-market approach. This has occurred as the result of pressure from the World Bank, the International Monetary Fund, and various Western donors, but also because these economies are now more developed and have more private resources and regional institutions that can help new businesses get started.

Stock traders at the Saudi Investment Bank in Riyadh work the phones inside the trade room. The Saudi stock market, Tadawul, is the largest in the Arab world. In December 2006, Tadawul dropped 20%, more than 8,000 points. Middle-class Saudis, many who sold their cars and spent their life savings to enter the market, were burned. In September 2007, Saudi Arabia opened its stock market to neighboring Gulf countries, without limit and in any industry, for the first time. They hope to eventually open the market to all foreign investors.

Also, as the Arab League countries get further away from their colonial past and gain security about their continued independence and nationhood, they are less concerned about the consequences of foreign ownership.

Many economic reforms and legal and institutional changes have to be made to allow a country to move in a free-market direction. This has been happening in the last decade. In 2000, the UAE set up a stock market. A year later Bahrain and Saudi Arabia took steps to improve the regulation of their stock markets and began to allow foreigners to trade stocks. Bahrain, Kuwait, Oman, Qatar, and Saudi Arabia began to allow for 100 percent-foreign ownership in most sectors of the economy (up from the noncontrolling 49 percent share which Bahrain used to allow). Bahrain and the UAE also made it easier for companies from outside the region to own buildings and lease land. Kuwait reduced tax rates from about 55 percent to 25 percent. Qatar removed limits on the amount of interest currency deposits could earn in local banks (at the same time it also strengthened bank supervision). The UAE established several free trade zones in which foreign companies can operate without having to

OVERCOMING RED TAPE

Under colonialism, countries were run by others. Once Arab countries gained independence, they wanted to be truly free but knew that to do so they would need to have complete control over their economies. So they put in place many regulations and tariffs to control the direction of economic development and the things that were exported and imported (so only the items the country really needed were allowed in because there was a shortage of foreign currency). Over time, these regulations became a mess of red tape that prevented economic growth.

Consider the case of Syria. In order to import goods into Syria the following are needed: (1) a bill of lading, (2) a valid import license, (3) a packing list in triplicate, (4) a certificate of origin in triplicate, (5) a letter from the corresponding bank, and (6) a commer-

conform to the country's regular labor, environmental, tax, health and safety regulations.[50]

Steps are also being taken to privatize many activities that used to be done by the state. For instance, in Bahrain, garbage collection is now done by private companies, and it plans similar moves in the transportation, telecommunications, postal, and tourism sectors. Oman has gone even further, allowing foreign companies to construct and run three power plants. It also is developing plans to sell off existing government-owned plants, as well as the management of its airports, and water and sewage treatment facilities. Saudi Arabia has targeted 20 state-run sectors to be privatized (sold off to private companies), including telecommunications, electricity, postal services, water, railroad, education, and air transportation.[51]

cial invoice in triplicate describing the types of goods. All of these must be certified by the Syrian Chamber of Commerce and the Syrian Embassy in the country of origin. Payment must be made by means of a documentary letter of credit. The exporter also needs to include two statements on the invoice: (1) whether the exporter has an agent in Syria, and (2) whether the company is in compliance with the league's boycott of Israel. Finally, the exporter should expect to pay a tariff of up to 150 percent, depending upon how necessary the government feels the product is to the country (as Syria has a non-convertible currency, foreign exchange can be difficult to come by and the government doesn't want it spent on unnecessary items).[*]

* "Trade Barriers," The PRS Group, October 1, 2006.

Some countries, however, are having trouble implementing parts of the GAFTA program. For instance, Lebanon has had a hard time finding ways to protect its new industries, and without that protection they could go bankrupt. Also, in 2007, intra-Arab trade was still only about 10 percent of the region's total trade (not quite twice what it was before GAFTA), and unemployment in the region remains high. These problems suggest that changes to GAFTA will need to be made to increase regional integration further.

INTEGRATING THE MIDDLE EAST AND NORTH AFRICA INTO GLOBAL TRADING NETWORKS

Since early in the twenty-first century, the Europeans and the Americans have been encouraging Arabs to expand their trade relationships with them, in addition to expanding trade within MENA. Since 2003 the United States has been pushing the league to enlarge GAFTA to include Turkey, Iran, and Israel by 2013. This idea would link trade to an Arab-Israeli peace process. President George W. Bush calls this plan the Greater Middle East Initiative, and the expanded trading region, the Middle East Free Trade Area (MEFTA). The plan is controversial not only because it includes Israel but also because MEFTA might exclude Comoros, Djibouti, Mauritania, Somalia, Sudan, and the Palestinian territories. Another part of the plan that is contentious is its "democratization" component. It is not surprising that in 2003, the league expressed reservations about the proposal, and as of the beginning of 2008 the idea has gone nowhere.

The Europeans want to create a Euro-Mediterranean free trade area that links the EU to some league countries. Since 1995, the EU has been pushing its Mediterranean Basin Initiative (MBI). The goal is to bring the six Arab states that border the Mediterranean Sea (Algeria, Egypt, Lebanon, Libya, Morocco, and Syria) into a closer economic and political relationship with the EU and to provide Europe with a skilled work force to offset its shrinking population. These six countries represent a $30 billion annual market for European goods and services, and all of them except Syria already have free trade agreements with the EU. Over a decade, MBI would eliminate trade and investment barriers between the two regions in manufactured goods.

In another move, the EU launched a series of talks with the Gulf Cooperation Council in 2000 aimed at eliminating barriers between itself and the GCC. The agreement does not give GCC states greater access to European markets than they already have, but they might agree to it because it could increase European financial and technical assistance, and this might increase the confidence of foreigners to invest in the region.

Over the past 60 years, the league has continually looked for ways to integrate the economies of the region in order to serve its larger goal of strengthening the cooperation and cohesion of the Arab world. This goal is important so that Arabs can take their place in the world and compete against the world's powerful economic and political players. This agenda is no less important today than it was six decades ago when the league was formed. In the differences between GAFTA, MEFTA, and MBI, the same tensions that have affected the Arab world since the colonial era are still evident. The West still wants to engage the Arab world in ways that strengthen its own economies, but this plan might not help the region as a whole. The choices that will be made in the next few years about GAFTA, MEFTA, and MBI—as well as choices about how the Arab world relates to the World Trade Organization—will be critical for the future economic development of the Arab world.

Arab Culture: Preservation and Change

At the beginning of the twenty-first century, the Arab world is changing fast. It has a young, urban population that is quick to embrace new technologies such as computers, the Internet, and cell phones.

Likely because of both the harsh natural environment and historical settlement patterns, this region is one of the most urbanized parts of the world, with between 60 percent and 85 percent of the population in each Arab country living in cities, the largest of which is Cairo, Egypt. This city has between 11 million and 20 million people. This makes it as big as Chicago or even New York City. Baghdad is another major city; before the Iraq war started in 2003, it had 5.9 million people. Other large cities include: Riyadh and Jeddah in Saudi Arabia; Khartoum, Sudan; Alexandria, Egypt; and Casablanca,

Many Arab countries are experiencing a digital revolution. The major advances in information and communication technologies, combined with the rapid growth of global networks have boosted the number of communications providers and customers entering both the fixed line and mobile markets. Telecommunications giant Nokia reported a 45.1 percent increase in cell phone sales, to 19.3 million devices in Africa and the Middle East in 2007.

Morocco. The percentage of the population that lives in cities is highest for the small countries of the Persian Gulf, with Kuwait topping the list at 97 percent. Egypt, the most populous country, had 45 percent of its population in cities in 1999. More typical are Tunisia, Algeria, and Lebanon, whose urban population range between 60 percent and 87 percent.[52]

The Middle East and North Africa is also a young region in that more than half of its population is younger than 20. This is one of the youngest populations in the world, which is important because young people are typically the first to use new technology.[53]

ARAB ADOPTION OF NEW COMMUNICATIONS TECHNOLOGY

COUNTRY	PERCENTAGE OF POPULATION WITH COMPUTERS	PERCENTAGE OF POPULATION WHO USE THE INTERNET	PERCENTAGE OF POPULATION WITH CELL PHONES	PERCENTAGE OF POPULATION WHO OWN TELEVISIONS
Algeria	0.9	2.6	84	98
Bahrain	∧	∧	∧	∧
Comoros	∧	∧	∧	∧
Djibouti	∧	∧	∧	∧
Egypt	3.2	5.4	91	95
Jordan	5.5	11.0	99	97
Kuwait	18.3	24.4	99	95
Lebanon	11.3	16.9	∧	93
Libya	2.4	3.6	∧	∧
Mauritania	2.1	1.4	∧	21
Morocco	2.1	11.7	95	76
Oman	4.7	9.7	∧	79
Palestine	∧	∧	∧	∧
Qatar	∧	∧	∧	∧
Saudi Arabia	35.4	6.6	92	99
Somalia	0.6	2.5	∧	8
Sudan	1.7	3.2	60	49
Syria	3.2	4.3	99	80
Tunisia	4.8	8.4	95	90
UAE	11.6	32.1	99	86
Yemen	1.5	0.9	68	43
USA	74.9	63.0	95	97
World	13.0	13.9	69	84

∧ denotes no data available

Source: *2006 World Development Indicators.* Washington, D.C.: The World Bank, 2006.

THE ANCIENT ROOTS OF ARAB CULTURE

In addition to being a dynamic culture, the Arab world is an ancient one. It is so old, in fact, that this region is often called the "cradle of civilization." It is the home of some of the world's oldest continuously inhabited human settlements. Egypt has one of the longest histories of any country on earth, with a written language that is 5,000 years old. The great pyramids of Egypt were built around 2,600 B.C., and recent dating suggests the Sphinx at Giza might be 10,000 years old! Records show that Egyptian pharaohs (kings) controlled Sudan (then called the "land of Kush") and were trading with Eritrea already in 3,000 B.C.

It is not just Egypt that has an ancient civilization. Iraq is the location of several of the world's first cities, including Ur, in southern Iraq, and Lagash, which grew between the Tigris and Euphrates rivers, where Baghdad is located today. Both of these ancient cities date to around 2,500 B.C. Syria boasts of having one of the world's oldest libraries, of clay tablets, which tells of the ancient city of Elba that existed more than 4,000 years ago. Out of these cities came some of the world's first powerful empires: the Sumerian, the Babylonian, and the Assyrian. Later, this area was central to the empires of the Greeks, Romans, Persians, Ottomans, and eventually the British and the French.

Arab scholars have made important contributions to mathematics, inventing the Arabic numerals that we use as our numbers in the West. They also invented algebra (*al-jabr* in Arabic), which means the science of the "reunion of broken parts."

The cultural similarities across the region date to the arrival of Islam between A.D. 630 and 700. Islam created a unified cultural and trading space that lasted until the era of European colonization. Islamic civilization in the Arab world also led to the flourishing of literature, architecture, art, music, philosophy, agriculture, medicine, astronomy, and navigation. For many centuries, the region led the world in the quality and number of its universities.

For a time, the development of Arab culture waned. This coincided with the decline of the Ottoman Empire and European powers moving into the region. Unlike the Ottomans who unified the Arab world, Europeans divided the region into a patchwork of colonies controlled by different European powers: Great Britain (Egypt, Iraq, Palestine, Saudi Arabia, Somalia, Sudan, the Trucial States, and Yemen); France (Algeria, Djibouti, Egypt, Lebanon, Morocco, Syria, and Tunisia); Italy (Eritrea and Libya); and Spain (Western Sahara). Each European colonizer imported its own system and language into its colonies, and this undermined traditional common bonds across the region. Although European colonization did not last long, typically only about 50–70 years, from the second-half or last-third of the nineteenth century until the end of World War I or World War II, it deeply transformed many Arab countries as their leaders and intellectuals got European educations, often by attending university in the major cities of Europe.

European colonization spurred different reactions among Arabs. Some preferred the influences of the West to the systems of the declining Ottoman Empire. Others rejected European influence as corrupting and dangerous, preferring Islamic traditions and promoting Pan-Islamic ideas to regenerate Arab civilization. Still others worked to combine ideas about nationalism, modernization, and independence which were prominent in Europe, with the new ideology of Arab nationalism. Arab nationalists hoped this would revive and modernize the region.

Enlivened by a new sense of Arab identity and a new vision of Arabs as one nation, Pan-Arabists delved into a vigorous re-examination of Arab culture, history, and language. These are the ideas that animated the formation of the Arab League, and part of its core mission since then has been to promote the preservation, restoration, and development of Arab culture.

THE CULTURAL TREATY OF THE ARAB LEAGUE

From its very beginning, central goals of the Arab League have been to preserve ancient Arab culture; to promote understanding of Arab culture in other parts of the world; to spur new developments in Arab civilization; and to improve education in the region. These goals are at the heart of the 1946 Cultural Treaty, one of the league's founding documents and its first regional treaty. This document frames how the Arab League should work on culture. A year later, the league held a cultural conference in Lebanon that focused on the need to cultivate the Arab national spirit and social consciousness, and promoted global trends toward unity, democracy, freedom, and equality. These ideas were endorsed by the League Council at its seventh meeting, held in 1948.

LEAGUE BODIES THAT WORK ON CULTURE

Next the league set up a Permanent Cultural Committee, as well as a Cultural and Social Affairs Department. More recently, it has added departments within the secretary-general's office to deal with women's issues and children's issues.

The league also set up specialized institutes. One of these is the Institute for the Revival of Arabic Manuscripts, which makes manuscripts available to public and to private collections. To do this, it collected thousands of manuscripts from all over the region and Europe, and in the days before personal computers, it copied them onto microfilm.

The treaty also talks about sharing resources among the region's museums and libraries. The league also works to set up museums and trains Arabs to preserve historical artifacts. For instance, in 2002, the league helped sponsor a month-long workshop that brought 20 young people from nine countries to the Juma Al Majid Center for Culture and Heritage in Dubai to learn the art of manuscript restoration. They also learned the Islamic art of binding books.

Another specialized center is the Institute of Higher Arab Studies in Cairo, set up in 1953 to train Arabs in law, history, geography, and social sciences. This institute publishes many journals on these subjects. Other such institutions include: the Arab Academy for Science & Technology; the Institute of Arab Studies;

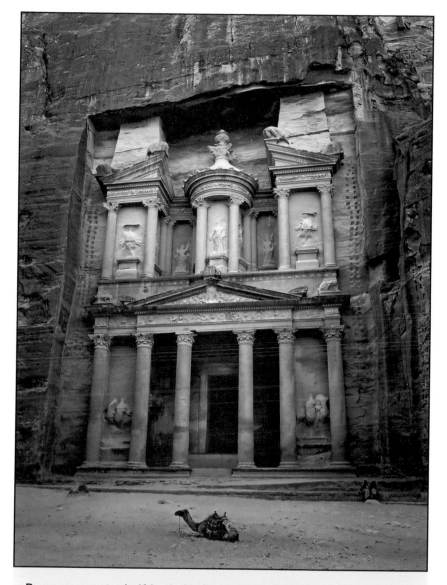

Petra, a vast city half-built, half-carved into dusky-pink rock more than 2000 years ago, was an important trade route that linked China, India, and southern Arabia with Egypt, Syria, Greece, and Rome. Today it is Jordan's most valuable treasure and greatest tourist attraction. UNESCO has described it as "one of the most precious cultural properties of man's cultural heritage," and declared it a World Heritage Site in 1985.

and the Baghdad Music Academy. There is also the Higher Arab Institute for Translation, which is charged with translating the world's great modern and classical books into Arabic, in order to help Arabs know the wider world. It also is supposed to facilitate the translation of important Arab books into other languages, in order to promote understanding of Arabs in the rest of the world. In line with this goal, in 1999, the Arab League Educational, Cultural and Scientific Organization (ALECSO), gave a collection of 100 Arabic publications to the library of the Oriental Institute of the Czech Republic.[54]

ALECSO, which was established in 1967 in Tunis, is the league's main body, dealing with cultural and educational issues. It hosts special conferences in various cultural, scientific, and educational areas, which bring together experts to exchange ideas and discuss solutions to common problems. Often what comes out of these meetings is a new regional professional association that then sets up a program to develop the ideas that were generated at the conference. During its first 20 years, the league sponsored six conferences on education, four archaeology conferences, four teachers' conferences, and several conferences each for writers, journalists, doctors, and lawyers.[55]

Another way ALECSO is helping preserve the region's heritage is through uniting with the United Nations Educational, Scientific and Cultural Organization's (UNESCO) World Cultural Heritage Sites program. Together they work to protect and restore such sites. This collaboration has resulted in the designation of 55 locations in the Arab world as World Heritage Sites (out of 853 sites worldwide). Morocco alone has eight sites.

PROMOTING CULTURAL EXCHANGE

The Cultural Treaty also charges the league with promoting exchanges among ordinary people in the region so they can gain a broader idea about what it means to be Arab. This includes exchanges of teachers and students, as well as scouting and sport exchanges.

The World Organization of Scout Movement has over 20 million members, which includes Boy Scouts, Girl Scouts, and adult leaders in 216 countries. In Lebanon, where these Boy Scouts are performing drills before a day trip, there are over 80,000 scouts and guides in 20 different scout associations.

In 1953, the league held the first Pan-Arab Games in Alexandria, Egypt. Originally planned to occur every four years, they sometimes had to be postponed for political reasons. In the last 40 years they have been held more regularly. The Pan-Arab Games bring together male and female athletes to compete in a spirit of friendship. The eleventh Games occurred in Egypt in November 2007. Featured among the 32 events for men and 24 for women were track and field, soccer, basketball, handball, volleyball, water polo, horse jumping, rifle marksmanship, karate, and gymnastics. In the 2007 games about 7,000 athletes from all 22 league countries participated. The next games are scheduled to take place in Lebanon in 2011. The league has also run training programs for coaches across the region.

The league has promoted the development of Arab youth by encouraging the establishment of Boy Scout and Girl Scout chapters. Since scouting started for boys in England in 1907, it has grown into a worldwide organization that in 2008 had 155 national Boy Scout and 144 national Girl Scout organizations. Together they have a membership of over 20 million youth. In 2008, all league members (except Djibouti, Somalia, and Eritrea, but including the Occupied Territories) had Boy Scout organizations. Twelve members had Girl Scouts. The activities of both groups are coordinated by the Arab Scout Regional Office in Egypt, one of six regional offices of the World Organization of Scout Movement.

In addition to traditional activities such as camping, outdoor survival skills, and leadership development, today scouting encourages young people to work on adolescent health, community development, working toward peace, relief work, human rights, etc.[56] Scouting also provides an opportunity for young people to travel to international youth gatherings. At the seventh inter-regional gathering, held in Tunisia in 2006, Boy Scout organizations from Europe and MENA worked on overcoming prejudices and spreading peace by forming permanent cross-regional partnerships to work on joint projects such as "Rebirth of the Phoenix." The Lebanese scouts set this up to provide a way for other scouts to join them in reconstructing their country in the wake of war. It involves young people around the world in a chain of solidarity, mobilizing financial resources and volunteers for rebuilding infrastructure, for environmental and health campaigns, and for educational programs for families, children, and injured people.[57]

Children and the Arab League

THE LEAGUE WORKS IN MANY WAYS TO IMPROVE THE LIVES OF children. In addition to sponsoring the sporting and scouting events that were discussed in the last chapter, it works to improve education. The league also promotes child health and the rights of children. The league has even been involved in supporting the development of an Arab doll!

PROMOTING EDUCATION

The Cultural Treaty addresses how the league can work on education. It promotes having all member states use the same lesson plans, train teachers in similar methods, and grant the same types of graduation degrees. This standardization is designed to make teacher and student exchanges easier and to allow people who graduate in one country to work in another.

AN ARAB ALTERNATIVE TO BARBIE

Girls everywhere like to play with Barbie, the world's most famous doll. Barbie, however, is not for everyone. Not only does Barbie have skimpy clothing, she also has a boyfriend, and she drinks champagne.

For many Arab parents, this means Barbie is not a good role model for their daughters. Until recently, however, Arab parents had nothing else to offer. That is, until Dr. Abla Ibrahiem, an official in the Arab League's Department of Childhood, in 1999 developed Laila, following the advice of children who participated in the 1998 Arab League's children's celebration.

The Laila doll has a brother, Dara, and a best friend Sara. According to Dr. Ibrahiem, Laila is a "representative Arab girl."

She has wavy black hair and dark eyes, and she "wouldn't be caught dead in a miniskirt." Laila prefers to hang out with her brother and best friend, rather than a boyfriend.

Laila and her gang have both Western-style outfits and traditional folk dresses from Egypt, Syria, and other Arab countries.

Arab governments put a lot of money behind the doll and the league lobbied the region's toy

(continues)

(continued)

makers to manufacture Laila, with the result that she is made in Cairo and sells for about $10. Since the development of Laila, other toy manufacturers have begun to develop other dolls that fit better with Arab culture. A popular one is Fulla, who is sold with accessories, such as umbrellas, bikes, cameras, and inflatable chairs. She is designed to be a traditional Muslim girl. More than 1.3 million Fulla dolls have been sold.

Another goal of the Cultural Treaty was to develop an Arab-centered curriculum in history, geography, and literature, to replace the colonial-era textbooks. Under the old curriculum, Arab students were mainly taught dates and events that affected European countries, and they learned about these events from a Western point of view. Now students are taught about the events that are most important to the development of the Arab world, and these events are explained from an Arab point of view.

Since 1950 the league has published information about the region's educational systems in an effort to get the information necessary to meet the educational goals in the Cultural Treaty. Since the late 1980s, ALECSO has been working with UNICEF on these studies.

MEASURING PROGRESS IN EDUCATION

There are two important ways to measure how well a country (or region) is doing in education. One is to look at what percentage of people can read. This is called the literacy rate. In the Arab world, the literacy rate of people between ages 15 and 24 has increased from 45 percent in 1970 to 78 percent in the early 2000s. This is one of the best rates of improvement in the world.

Another way to measure education is to look at the percentage of children who go to school. Since gaining independence, Arab states have worked hard to promote free or nearly free public education and this has had good results. In 1990, the region had 78 percent of its children in school. By 2004, this had grown to 88 percent (though there is a declining rate for boys).[58] Even with this improvement, in 2006 more than 10 million Arab children were not in school, especially in Egypt, Iraq, Morocco, and Sudan. Other states are doing better, especially Tunisia, where 99 children out of 100 go to school.

It is not traditional for Arab children to go to preschool because most families have an adult at home during the day. Only about 16 percent (or one in six) of Arab children attended preschool in 2006. But this is growing as more women begin to work outside the home.

THE STRUCTURE OF SCHOOLING

In all Arab countries, education after primary school continues for about six years. Then students move on to secondary school, which is divided into two parts. The first part of secondary school lasts for three years. During this stage, students finish the basic education they started in primary school but with a bit more specialization.

Students typically start the second stage of secondary school when they are 15 or 16. During these three years, students specialize in either general, technical, or vocational studies. Students must complete the general or technical studies to go to college. The vocational curriculum is for students who want to learn a trade, like plumbing. About 95 percent of students do the general curriculum; however, only 60 percent of all students in the region go to the second part of secondary school, though the percentages differ a lot by country. In Djibouti only about

15 percent go to the second half of secondary school, whereas in Bahrain 100 percent of students go.[59]

EDUCATION IN THE TWENTY-FIRST CENTURY

The studies of education done by UNESCO and ALECSO don't just count how many students are studying—they also suggest how to improve education in the Arab world. Recent reports have identified 10 changes that should be made to make education more available and better for all children. To start, more schools need to be built, and more than 450,000 more teachers need to be trained immediately if the Arab region is to achieve the UN Millennium Development goal of getting all children a primary school education by 2015. There especially is a lack of female teachers in rural areas, and this is discouraging girls from participating in the classroom and finishing school. To recruit additional teachers, salaries should be raised so more people will want to become teachers. It also recommends that teachers be trained to teach in ways that encourage students to learn and become good problem solvers. Regional centers should be given more resources so they can do this training and help schools in other ways. What is being taught (the curriculum) also needs to change and be updated, to include human rights and other topics. Other recommendations concern helping local communities find new ways to pay for their schools, and encouraging the 12 Arab countries that don't yet have ministries of education to create them to help these governments improve education. The last two suggestions are to eliminate school fees so poor children can attend school for free, and to improve transportation so children can easily get to school.

Colleges and universities in the Arab world also need to improve. New teaching methods need to be introduced so students learn to think critically. The schools need more computers and other information technology. They also need to provide their students with more job preparation and with

The Al-Shati primary school in the Gaza refugee camp of Al-Shati in the Occupied Territories has installed computers and a wireless network that connects all its schools and introduced information technology as a new subject. On January 27, 2008, Microsoft Chairman Bill Gates announced a partnership with the Mohammed bin Rashid Foundation to enhance research and knowledge creation in the Arab world, acknowledging the critical role that information and communication technology plays in creating a vibrant economy.

more training in writing and speaking English, which is the world's language of business. And they need to invest more in scientific research.[60] In 2001, the Arab nations together only spent about 0.5 percent of their GDP on research and development; this is far below the global average of 1.4 percent.[61]

One exciting development in college education with which ALECSO is assisting is the growing use of "distance learning." In this approach, students do not go to a school building to take classes; rather, they listen to lectures on TV, radio, or computer, and communicate with their professors through e-mail. This is improving the access to, and quality of, college education, especially for women (who in the Arabian Peninsula and Maghreb face cultural restrictions on attending school alongside men). It also helps young people who do not live near universities.

CHILDREN'S HEALTH

In addition to education, another important issue facing Arab children is health. Each year, 500,000 children in the region die before their first birthday. Four million children have not been vaccinated against measles. Seven million children don't get enough to eat.

There are also several million children in the region who are living in war zones. Then there are about 13 million children who must work. More than half of these working children don't go to school.

The main ways the league works on youth issues are through its various bodies devoted to children's issues, such as the Arab Children Technical and Consultation Committee, the Office of the Director-General of Women and Children, and the league's administration that is devoted to family and childhood. The league also discusses children's issues at its annual summits.

THE MILLENNIUM GOALS AND ARAB CHILDREN

At its 2003 summit in Beirut, the league adopted the "Arab World Fit for Children" document, which is modeled on UNICEF's "A World Fit for Children" report that was written to provide governments with advice on how achieve the UN Millennium Development Goals by 2015. These goals were established in 2000 to help countries focus on the world's worst problems. The goals are to: (1) eradicate extreme poverty and hunger; (2) achieve universal primary education; (3) promote gender equality and empower women; (4) reduce child mortality by two-thirds; (5) improve the health of mothers; (6) combat HIV/AIDS, malaria and tuberculosis; (7) ensure environmental sustainability; and (8) develop a global partnership for development.[62] Each country has since written a report that sets its own targets for meeting these general goals and the methods it will use to do so. For example, in the Arab world "reducing child mortality [death] by two thirds" means cutting the number of children who die before their fifth birthday, from about 8 children out of every 100 children (as was the case in 1990) to less than 3 children out of every 100 in 2015. The main ways they have proposed to do this are to increase the number of women who see a doctor while they are pregnant, and to increase the use of vaccinations once the children are born.

Some other ways in which league countries are trying to meet the child targets in the millennium goals are demonstrated by Qatar, which has developed a "Child Rights Culture" curriculum in its schools through which students are taught the rights they have under the Convention on the Rights of the Child, and how these are related to the rights granted to children within Islam. They are also demonstrated by Syria that in 2005 set up "friendly spaces" in Palestinian refugee camps where teens can hang out in a safe place.[63]

The league also holds youth forums for children from all over the region. These have cultural activities that promote Arab identity and values. At these meetings, children also discuss the problems facing youth. For instance, at the forum held in Amman, Jordan, in 2000, 100 children from 16 countries put together their own "call for action," asking for better teaching and for the media to put out better images of young people. Finally, the league sponsors child-focused conferences at which experts gather to discuss how to solve the problems facing young people. So, not only by preserving the culture of the past but also by promoting the needs of the region's youth, the league is helping the region preserve and promote its culture.

9

Evaluating
the Impact
of the League

OFTEN PEOPLE ASK IF A REGIONAL ORGANIZATION IS EFFECTIVE or not. To answer this question, it is helpful to think about how much power an organization has, and how that power is arranged. Centralized organizations whose power is located all in one place can act quickly and decisively, and for that reason such organizations can easily put an agenda into action. The inability to act quickly and decisively is the main reason the United States replaced its original Articles of Confederation with the Constitution of the United States. As a confederation, the original 13 American colonies acted together as a congress, but each kept their own "sovereignty, freedom and independence," for there really was no power above those colonies, as the Congress could only act when 9 of the 13 colonies were in agreement.

The Arab League is an organization which operates like a confederation in that its highest body is the council, in which each sovereign member state has one vote. The League Council is even stricter than the Congress of the U.S. Confederation because it requires an unanimous vote to act on all important matters. This extraordinarily tough standard means that in many areas the league simply can't act, given all the differences between its members. In light of these limitations, one could argue the league has been able to accomplish a lot. However, if judged by what the region actually needs, many have argued it is an ineffective organization. When it has added new bodies, the league has adopted a less tough majority voting rule, and in this way it is making small steps toward creating a system more capable of action. However, the member states as of 2008 have not adopted the current secretary-general's recommendation that the council lower its voting rule to a mere majority.

Another way to think about whether an organization is successful is to consider whether it can achieve its main goals. In the case of the league, its main goals are to prevent foreign domination and to enhance Arab power, security, prosperity, and culture. The league's effectiveness on security issues has not been very high. For this reason, it has been called "a toothless tiger." At a 2006 regional debate sponsored by the Qatar Foundation, the league was criticized by a Lebanese presidential candidate, reflecting the views of many Arabs, as being "inefficient, counter-productive, a sham and corrupt." At the end of the debate, 60 percent of the audience voted in favor of closing the league down, arguing that it fails to protect human rights and it fails to speak out against oppression. At that same event, however, a league staff member argued the league cannot be blamed for the fact that the governments of its member states are not reforming themselves.[64]

Others defend the league by arguing that its lack of success in many areas is due to the problems it faces, including the Arab/Israeli conflict, countries in which governments have fallen apart (known as failed states), and the frequent interference of powerful outside states, initially during the Cold War, then because of the importance of oil, and more recently because of the War on Terrorism.

In a 2003 interview, the Arab League's secretary-general, Amr Moussa, was asked if he thought the league had let Arabs down. He replied, "There is a sense of this . . . a feeling that the League has not done its job properly. We are trying to revive the Arab League." When asked how he is doing that, he replied, "By working on the social, economic, and technical issues. By working on education, health, and other issues."[65] In other words, by working on issues other than politics.

The league plays an important role in raising Arab concerns to other governments, and at UN and regional organizations. The league is also making strides in regional trade and in coordinating other economic areas. At its 2006 summit, Arab leaders agreed to collaborate more closely on research and to increase funding to develop science and technology. The league is helping to establish region-wide educational standards and curriculum, and it is facilitating teacher training. It also is working on cultural preservation. Even in these cases, however, there is a concern that the league has been long on talk and short on action, for it is unclear in many cases whether the good ideas that can be found in the reports that come out of the various conferences which the league holds get translated into concrete actions.

In summary, although the Arab League does have its problems, it is unlikely that the region can do without it. As is sometimes said about other organizations, such as the United Nations, if the Arab League didn't exist, it would need to be invented, because the areas in which it works are too important to be ignored and too widespread to be handled by the individual governments in the region.

CHRONOLOGY

1913	First Arab Congress meets in Paris to call for autonomy for Arabs within the Ottoman Empire.
1914	Ottoman Empire enters World War I on side of Germany.
1915	Arab nationalist leaders send the Damascus Protocol to Hussein supporting his idea for an Arab revolt against the Ottoman Empire.
1915–1916	Hussein-McMahon Correspondence.
1916	Sykes-Picot Agreement signed between France and Great Britain; Arab revolt against Ottoman Rule begins.
1917	Balfour Declaration of support for the creation of the state of Israel.
1922	End of the Ottoman Empire and beginning of the Mandate System (which lasted until 1948).
1932	Nazis come to power in Germany.
1936	Palestine Revolt (lasts until 1939).
1939	London Round Table Conference meeting to consider fate of Palestine.
1941	British government announces support for greater Arab unity.
1943	Great Britain repeats pledge of support for Arab unity. United States supports the idea of an Arab organization.
1944	United States reiterates its support for the formation of an Arab organization. Leaders from Iraq, Transjordan, Saudi Arabia, Syria, Lebanon, and Yemen meet in Alexandria, Egypt, to discuss the formation of an Arab organization. Alexandria Protocol is issued.

1945   Arab leaders at the Pan Arab Conference sign the Charter of the League of Arab States, creating the Arab League.

United Nations is created.

Arab League begins the boycott of Israeli goods, which lasts until 1995.

1946   Signing of the Cultural Treaty of the Arab League.

1947   United Nations Partition Plan for Palestine approved.

1948   State of Israel created.

Arab states declare war on Israel.

1949   Joint Defense and Economic Cooperation Treaty (JDEC).

1950   Joint Defense Council (JDC) of the Arab League created.

1953   Economic and Social Council established.

1956   Suez Crisis begins.

1957   Formation of the Council for Arab Economic Unity.

1959   Arab Development Bank (later known as the Arab Financial Organization) set up.

1964   Recognition of the Palestine Liberation Organization (PLO) by the Arab League.

1965   Arab Common Market established.

1967   Six-Day War fought between Israel and Arab neighbors Egypt, Jordan, and Syria, with the contribution of troops and arms to Arab forces by Iraq, Saudi Arabia, Kuwait, and Algeria.

Formation of Arab League Educational, Cultural and Scientific Organization (ALECSO).

1973   Yom Kippur War.

Arab League recognizes the PLO as the only legitimate representative of the Palestinian people.

1980   Egypt expelled from the Arab League for signing separate peace agreement with Israel.

Strategy for Joint Arab Economic Action (JAEA) is launched.

1981   Formation of the Cooperation Council of the Arab States of the Gulf, also known as the Gulf Cooperation Council (GCC).

1982   Israel invades Lebanon.

1987–1993   First *Intifada* takes place between Palestinian civilians and Israeli forces.

1989   Formation of the Union of the Arab Maghreb (UAM).

Formation of the Arab Cooperation Council (ACC).

1990   Iraq invades Kuwait and begins the Gulf War.

Federation of North and South Yemen.

2001   Amr Moussa becomes secretary-general of the Arab League.

2003   United States invades Iraq and starts the Iraq War.

2005   Greater Arab Free Trade Agreement (GAFTA) put fully into effect.

2007   Arab Parliament is formed.

NOTES

Chapter 2

1. M. F. Anabtawi, *Arab Unity in Terms of Law.* The Hague: Martinus Nijhoff, 1963, 41–42.
2. "The 1936 Riots," Jewish Virtual Library-The American-Israeli Cooperative Enterprise. October 11, 2007. Available online at *http://www.jewishvirtuallibrary.org/jsource/History/riots36.html.*
3. Quoted in George E. Kirk, *Middle East in the War.* London: Oxford University Press, 1952, 334.
4. Nuri al-Sa'id, "Arab Independence and Unity, A Note on Arab Independence and Unity with Particular Reference to Palestine and Suggestions for a Final Solution," From Muhammad Khalil's *The Arab States and the Arab League: A Documentary Record.* Beirut: Khayats, No. 4 (1962), 9–12.
5. The Arab League, "The Alexandria Protocol." October 7, 1944.
6. Ibid.
7. Robert W. Macdonald, *The League of Arab States: A Study in the Dynamics of Regional Organization.* Princeton: Princeton University Press, 1965, 41.
8. Anabtawi, 64.
9. The Arab League, "The Charter of the Arab League," Article II. March 22, 1945.
10. Anabtawi, 41–42.
11. Michael C. Hudson, ed., *Middle East Dilemma: The Politics and Economics of Arab Integration.* New York: Columbia University Press, 1999, 25.

Chapter 3

12. "Arab League Summit Adopts 'Algiers Declaration,'" British Broadcasting Corporation. March 23, 2005.

13. "League of Arab States," *The Middle East and North Africa 2005*. 51st Edition. London and New York: Europa Publications, 2005, 1358–1363.

Chapter 4

14. "The Balfour Declaration (1917)," Paul Brians and Mary Gallwey. Reading About the World. Volume 2, 3rd Edition. Harcourt Brace Custom Publishing, 1999.
15. Roy R. Andersen, Robert F. Seibert and Jon G. Wagner. *Politics and Change in the Middle East: Source of Conflict and Accommodation*. 4th edition. Englewood Cliffs: Prentice Hall, 1993, 84.
16. Andersen, 85.
17. Ibid., 74–75.
18. "World Wars: Genocide Under the Nazis," *Persecution to Genocide*. Available online at *http://www.bbc.co.uk/history/worldwars/genocide/radicalisation_01.shtml*.
19. "Palestine Royal (Peel) Commission Report, July 1937," Reproduced as Document 4.2 in Charles D. Smith *Palestine and the Arab-Israeli Conflict: A History with Documents*, 4th Edition. New York: Bedford/St. Martin's, 2001, 158–162.
20. Macdonald, 86.
21. Anabtawi, 43–44.
22. Macdonald, 91–93.
23. Ibid., 87.
24. Mitchell Bard, "The Arab Boycott," Jewish Virtual Library, The American-Israeli Cooperative Enterprise, October 11, 2007. Available online at *http://www.jewishvirtuallibrary.org/jsource/History/Arab_boycott.html*.
25. Tim McGirk. "Soft Drink Fizz Goes Flat in Gaza," *Time*, December 13, 2007. Available online at *http://www.time.com/time/magazine/article/0,9171,1694477,00.html*.

26. Macdonald, 89.
27. Ibid., 119–120.
28. Anderson, 120–121.
29. Smith, 421.
30. Anderson, 130.
31. "Israeli Spokesman Says Saudi Plan Non-Starter," *BBC Monitoring International Reports,* March 29, 2002.
32. Sana Aftab Khan, "Gaza Border Closures Accompanied by Fears of Humanitarian Crisis," *UN Chronicle On Line.* Available online at *http://www.un.org/Pubs/chronicle/2007/webArticles/080207_gazaborder.htm.*
33. Anderson, 125.

Chapter 5

34. Roger Owen, "Inter-Arab Economic Relations During the Twentieth Century: World Market vs. Regional Market?" *Middle East Dilemma: The Politics and Economics of Arab Integration*, Michael C. Hudson, ed. New York: Columbia University Press, 1999, 219; and Macdonald, 193.
35. Ugo Fasano and Zubair Iqbal, *GCC Countries: From Oil Dependence to Diversification.* International Monetary Fund, 2003.
36. Yusif A. Sayigh, "Arab Economic Integration: The Poor Harvest of the 1980s," *The Middle East Dilemma*, 245.
37. Fasano and Iqbal, GCC Countries.
38. Sayigh, 243.
39. Ibid., 244.
40. The World Bank, World Development Indicators Database, September 14, 2007. Available online at *http://siteresources.worldbank.org/DATASTATISTICS/Resources/GNIPC.pdf*; The World Bank *2007 Economic Developments and Prospects: Job Creation in an Era of High Growth, the Middle East and North Africa Region*, 2007. Available online at *http://siteresources.worldbank.*

org/INTMENA/Resources/EDP_2007_REPORT_Aug7.
pdf; and *The CIA World Fact Book 2007*. Available
online at *https://www.cia.gov/library/publications/the-
world-factbook/*.

Chapter 6

41. "League of Arab States," 1360.
42. Sayigh, 239.
43. "Arab League Collapse Carries Steep Economic Price,"
     The Middle East, May 2004, 29–31.
44. Ibid.
45. Sayigh, 246.
46. Ibid.
47. Delegation of the European Commission in Egypt, May
     2006, "Regional integration Arrangements–Mediterranean
     region." Available online at *http://www.delegy.ec.europa.eu/
     en/EU-Egypt_Trade_issues/Docs/Regional%20Integration%
     20Arrangements7.doc*.
48. "Egypt Minister Rashid to Champion Inter-Arab Trade
     as a Stepping Stone to Global Integration," *Financial
     Times Information*, May 18, 2006.
49. "Jordan GAFTA Absorbs 42.6% of Exports," *Financial
     Times Information*, August 10, 2006. Available online at
     the Global News Wire–Asia Africa Intelligence Wire,
     Infoprod. "Jordan GAFTA Controls 36.1% of Imports,"
     Financial Times Information, August 10, 2006. Available
     online at the Global News Wire–Asia Africa Intelligence
     Wire, Infoprod.
50. Fasano and Iqbal.
51. Ibid.

Chapter 7

52. UNESCO Institute for Statistics, "Arab States Regional
     Report." Montreal: UNESCO Institute for Statistics, 2002.

53. The World Bank, "2006 World Development Indicators."
     Washington, D.C.: The World Bank, 2006.
54. Academy of Sciences of the Czech Republic, "Oriental
     Institute Annual Report 1999." Available online at *http://
     www.orient.cas.cz/ou/anual/OU%201999.htm*.
55. Macdonald, 174–178.
56. World Federation of Scouts. Available online at *http://
     world.scout.org/satw/links.shtml; and http://www.wagggs
     world.org/en/about*.
57. World Federation of Scouts. Available online at *http://
     www.scout.org/es/information_events/news/2006/euro_
     arab_meeting_united_towards_a_culture_of_peace*.

Chapter 8
58. The World Bank 2006, 42.
59. UNESCO Institute for Statistics, 40–44.
60. Ibid.
61. Arab Human Development Report 2002, "Arab Human
     Development Lags Behind," The MENA Business Reports,
     July 3, 2002.
62. United Nations, "What are the Millennium Development
     Goals?" Available online at *http://www.un.org/millennium
     goals/*.
63. Ban-Ki Moon, "Children and the UN Millennium De-
     velopment Goals: Progress Toward A World Fit for Chil-
     dren." Available online at *http://www.unicef.org/worldfit
     forchildren/files/Children_and_the_MDGs_Final_EN.pdf*.

Chapter 9
64. "It is Time for the Arab League to Disband," The Doha
     Debates of the Qatar Foundation.
65. "Interview: Amr Moussa, Arab League," *Ame Info*. Avail-
     able online at *http://www.ameinfo.com/news/Detailed/
     16708.html*.

Academy of Sciences of the Czech Republic. *Oriental Institute Annual Report 1999.* Available online. URL: http://www. orient.cas.cz/ou/anual/OU%201999.htm.

AME Info. "Interview: Amr Moussa, Arab League," March 15, 2003. Available online. URL: http://www.ameinfo.com/ news/Detailed/16708.html.

Anabtawi, M. F. *Arab Unity in Terms of Law.* The Hague: Martinus Nijhoff, 1963.

Andersen, Roy R., Robert F. Siebert, and John G. Wagner. *Politics and Change in the Middle East: Source of Conflicts and Accommodation*, 4th ed. Englewood Cliffs, NJ: Prentice Hall, 1993.

Bard, Mitchell. "The Arab Boycott," Jewish Virtual Library- The American-Israeli Cooperative Enterprise. Available online. URL: http://www.jewishvirtuallibrary.org/jsource/ History/Arab_boycott.html.

BBC Monitoring International Reports. "Israeli Spokesman Says Saudi Plan Non-Starter," March 29, 2002.

Brians, Paul, and Mary Gallwey. "The Balfour Declaration (1917)," *Reading about the World*, Volume 2, (3rd Edition). New York: Harcourt Brace, 1999.

British Broadcasting Cooperation. "Arab League Summit Adopts 'Algiers Declaration,'" March 23, 2007.

Central Intelligence Agency. *The CIA World Fact Book 2007.* Available online. URL: https://www.cia.gov/library/ publications/the-world-factbook/.

Cesarani, David. "World Wars: Genocide Under the Nazis." *From Persecution to Genocide*). Available online. URL: http:// www.bbc.co.uk/history/worldwars/genocide/radicalisation_ 01.shtml.

Delegation of the European Commission in Egypt. "Regional integration Arrangements-Mediterranean region," Available online. URL: http://www.delegy.ec.europa.eu/en/EUEgypt_Trade_issues/Docs/Regional%20Integration%20Arrangements7.doc.

Fasano, Ugo, and Zubair Iqbal. "GCC Countries: From Oil Dependence to Diversification." International Monetary Fund, 2003.

Financial Times Information. "Egypt Minister Rashid to Champion Inter-Arab Trade As a Stepping Stone to Global Integration," May 18, 2006.

———. "Inter-Arab Trade Still Below Expectations." Global News Wire, May 9, 2007

———. "Jordan GAFTA Absorbs 42.6% of Exports," Global News Wire-Asia Africa Intelligence Wire, August 10, 2006.

———. "Jordan GAFTA Controls 36.1% of Imports," Global News Wire-Asia Africa Intelligence Wire, August 10, 2006.

Hudson, Michael C., ed. *Middle East Dilemma: The Politics and Economics of Arab Integration*. New York: Columbia University Press, 1999.

Jewish Virtual Library- The American-Israeli Cooperative Enterprise. "The 1936 Riots," October 11, 2007.

Khalil, Muhammed. *The Arab States and the Arab League: a Documentary Record*. Beirut: Khayats, 1962.

Khan, Sana Aftab. "Gaza Border Closures Accompanied by Fears of Humanitarian Crisis," *UN Chronicle On Line*. Available online. URL: http://www.un.org/Pubs/chronicle/2007/webArticles/080207_gazaborder.htm.

Kirk, George. *The Middle East in the War*. London: Oxford University Press, 1953.

"League of Arab States." *The Middle East and North Africa*. London: Taylor and Francis Group, 2005.

Macdonald, Robert D. *The League of Arab States: a Study in the Dynamics of Regional Organization.* Princeton: Princeton University Press, 1965.

Martin, Josh. "Arab League Collapse Carries Steep Economic Price," *The Middle East,* May 2004. Available online. URL: http://goliath.ecnext.com/coms2/gi_0199-64175/Arab-league-collapse-carries-steep.html.

McGirk, Tim. "Soft Drink Fizz Goes Flat in Gaza," *Time.* December 13, 2007. Available online. URL: http://www.time.com/time/magazine/article/0,9171,1694477,00.html.

Moon, Ban-Ki. *Children and the UN Millennium Development Goals: Progress Toward A World Fit for Children.* UNICEF. Available online. URL: http://www.unicef.org/worldfitfor-children/files/Children_and_the_MDGs_Final_EN.pdf.

Owen, Roger. *Middle East Dilemma: the Politics and Economics of Arab Integration.* Ed., Michael C. Hudson. New York: Columbia University Press, 1999.

Smith, Charles W. *Palestine and the Arab-Israeli Conflict: a History with Documents.* 4th ed. Boston and New York: Bedford/St. Martin's, 2001.

The Doha Debates of the Qatar Foundation. "It is Time for the Arab League to Disband," April 25, 2006.

The MENA Business Reports. *Arab Human Development Report 2002*, as referred to in "Arab Human Development Lags Behind," July 3, 2002.

The PRS Group. "Trade Barriers." 1 Oct. 2006.

The World Bank. *World Development Indicators.* Washington, D.C.: The World Bank, 2006.

———. *Economic Developments and Prospects: Job Creation in an Era of High Growth, the Middle East and North Africa Region,* 2007. Available online. URL: http://siteresources.worldbank.org/INTMENA/Resources/EDP_2007_REPORT_Aug7.pdf.

————. *World Development Indicators Data Base.* September 14, 2007. Available online. URL: http://siteresources.worldbank. org/DATASTATISTICS/Resources/GNIPC.pdf.

UNESCO Institute for Statistics. *Arab States Regional Report.* Montreal: UNESCO Institute for Statistics, 2002.

UNICEF Middle East and North Africa Regional Office, "An Arab World Fit for Children: Mechanisms for Joint Arab Action and an Arab Common Position, 2001." Available online. URL:http://www.unicef.org.tn/medias/hlm/cdp_ 120104_en.pdf.

UNICEF—UN General Assembly Special Session on Children. Follow-Up to National Plans of Action for Children, "A World Fit for Children," May 10, 2002. Available online. URL: http://www.unicef.org/specialsession/wffc/.

United Nations. "What are the Millennium Development Goals?" *UN Millennium Development Goals,* UN Web Services, Department of Public Information, United Nations, 2008.

Barakat, Ibitisam. *Tasting the Sky: A Palestinian Childhood.* New York: Farrar Straus Giroux, 2007.

Boudalika, Litsa. *If You Could Be My Friend: Letters of Mervet Akram Sha'ban and Galit Fink.* Translated from French by Alison Landes. History and glossary by Ariel Cohen. New York: Orchard Books, 1998.

Ellis, Deborah. *Three Wishes: Palestinian & Israeli Children Speak.* Toronto: Groundwood Books, 2004.

Harik, Ramsay M. and Elsa Marston. *Women in the Middle East: Tradition and Change,* Revised Edition. New York: Franklin Watts, 2003.

Kort, Michael G. *The Handbook of the Middle East.* Breckenridge, Colo.: Twenty-First Century Books, 2002.

Marcovitz, Hal. *Heroes and Holy Places.* Broomall, PA.: Mason Crest Publishers, 2004.

Marston, Elsa. *Figs and Fate: Stories About Growing Up in the Arab World Today.* New York: George Braziller, 2005.

McCoy, Lisa. *Modern Middle East Nations and Their Strategic Place in the World: Facts and Figures About the Middle East.* Philadelphia: Mason Crest Publishers, 2004.

Moktefi, Mokhtar. *The Arabs in the Golden Age.* Illustrated by Veronique Ageorges. Translated by Mary Kae LaRose. Brookfield, Conn.: The Millbrook Press, 1992.

Peters, James. *Very Simple Arabic Script.* London: Stacey International, 2003.

Temple, Bob. *The Arab Americans.* Philadelphia: Mason Crest Publishers, 2003.

Yackley-Franken, Nicki. *Teens in Saudi Arabia.* Minneapolis: Compass Point Books, 2007.

WEB SITES

Official Site of the League of Arab States
http://www.arableagueonline.org/las/english/level1_en.jsp?level1_id=1

Arab League General Information
Has original League documents and links to many other useful sites.

http://faculty.winthrop.edu/haynese/mlas/al1.html

Model League of Arab States Program
For high school and university students to explore how the AL works and to develop leadership skills in simulations of Arab League summits. Similar to Model UN and other such programs.

http://www.ncusar.org/modelarableague

Middle East Studies programs
at US colleges and universities
http://mideast.wisc.edu/acadmeiclinks.htm

News from Arab countries:
http://www.middleeastnews.com

http://www.albawaba.com/.

http://ww.ameinfo.com/

Arab World Directory:
http://www.araboo.com

American Arab Anti-Discriminiation Committee
Specalizes in countering hate crimes and discrimination against Arab Americans.

http://www.adc.org

PAGE

10: Infobase Publishing

16: Erich Lessing/Art Resource, NY

21: AFP/Getty Images

29: © Bettmann/CORBIS

35: Associated Press

40: Associated Press

47: Associated Press

50: © Aladin Abdel Naby/ Reuters/Corbis

53: AFP/Getty Images

61: Getty Images

68: Associated Press

71: Associated Press

77: Associated Press

82: Associated Press

89: Getty Images

93: Associated Press

97: AFP/Getty Images

103: AFP/Getty Images

108: www.shutterstock.com

110: Getty Images

113: Associated Press

117: Getty Images

INDEX

ABOUT THE CONTRIBUTORS

Author **CRIS E. TOFFOLO** is associate professor of political science and the director of the Justice and Peace Studies program at the University of St. Thomas in Minnesota. She specializes in political theory and comparative Third World politics. She is the author of "Pakistan," in the *World Encyclopedia of Political Systems and Parties*. She works with Peace Jam, and for many years worked with Amnesty International. Toffolo has a Ph.D. from the University of Notre Dame, an M.A. from George Washington University, and a B.S. from Alma College. She has studied and taught around the world.

Series editor **PEGGY KAHN** is professor of Political Science at the University of Michigan-Flint. She teaches world and European politics. She has been a social studies volunteer in the Ann Arbor, Michigan, public schools and helps prepare college students to become social studies teachers. She has a Ph.D. in political science from the University of California, Berkeley, and a B.A. in history and government from Oberlin College.